FACE-*to*-FACE
APPEARANCES
from JESUS

FACE-*to*-FACE APPEARANCES *from* JESUS

The Ultimate Intimacy

DAVID E. TAYLOR

KINGDOM OF GOD GLOBAL CHURCH
20320 Superior Rd. Taylor, MI 48180

For more information on ordering products (books, CDs, DVDs, etc.) from David E. Taylor, and for information on the next Miracles in America Crusades happening around the world, call
1-877-843-4567

Or visit on the Internet: www.kingdomofgodglobalchurch.org

ISBN 13: 978-1-64815-004-3

For Worldwide Distribution, Printed in the U.S.A.

Dedication

To Jesus, my Best Friend
who is the very reason for my being,
who has stood with me through
the darkest times of my life.
To the person of the Holy Spirit,
who is also my Friend and closest companion.

Table of Contents

Introduction The Confirmation of This Book 11

Chapter 1 **The Appearance** 17

The First Face-to-Face Encounter With Jesus 19
Forever Changed 23
The Supernatural Heavens Invade My Room......27
The Waterfall Experience 36

Chapter 2 **He Promised in His Word to Come to You** 47

His Covenant With Us of Appearances 49
The Opportunity of a Lifetime 53
He Wants to Know You Face-to-Face 55
He Promises to Come to You 58
The Fellowship Revealed................................64

Chapter 3 **How to Become a Personal Face-to-Face Friend With Jesus** 75

Face-To-Face Friendship With Jesus 77

Jesus Appears to Me as the Head
of the Church 80
How to Become His Friend 100

Chapter 4   **His Personality** **115**

What He's Like in Person.............................117
Jesus Causes Me to Appear Before
Him Face-to-Face in Heaven 119
He's a Person of Royalty 127
Jesus Still Talks About His Hometown
of Nazareth 143
He's a Man of Few Words............................144

Chapter 5   **He Appears and Shows Me the Most Important
Thing About Him: His Heart** **147**

The Lamb King 149
Understanding His Priorities 156
The Lamb 160
Jesus Is a Meek Person 163
Jesus Appears in Different Forms 173

Chapter 6   **He's Very Affectionate Toward Us** **175**

He Will Provoke You to Jealousy Just
to See Your Love for Him............................177
Intimacy Driven 182
He's A Person Who Loves His Enemies
Deeply...Even Judas 192
Taken to See Jerusalem in Jesus' Time 192
He's a Person of Love 195
Loving Our Enemies 198
What I've Seen of Jesus...............................199

Chapter 7   **He Is a Morning Person** **203**

Check His Countenance 211

The Revelation of the Morning Times 221
Understanding That God's Timing and
Schedule Are Different From Ours 222
Morning Visitations 225
His Significant Works Are Done
by Morning 227
Visited Every Morning 228
The Things That Belong to You When
Jesus Visits in the Morning 230
Benefits of Different Types of Visitations
From the Lord....................................230
Things That Belong to Your Peace in
the Morning Time Visitation 231
The Wings of the Morning 234

Chapter Reference: Jesus' Purpose for Appearing 237
Visitations Versus Appearances...................246
Appearances Can Happen In Many Ways 246
Wisdom Concerning Appearances 252

The Confirmation of This Book

In the process of writing this book, I received two major confirmations from the Lord that this was the time to write, finish, and release this message. The first came during the month of September in 2008. I was asleep, and I heard a voice saying, *"I want you to be finished with the book on face-to-face appearances by December."* Then suddenly I awoke. I knew this was the voice of the Lord speaking to me. He was giving me a deadline on a book (which, may I add, He had never done before). The second confirmation came during the preparation of this book. From September until December 1, 2008, the Lord supernaturally graced me to put down on paper almost every experience that He wanted in this book! That in itself is a miracle, and I give Him thanks. But the second confirmation came from one of my staff who was helping me type this book so that it would be ready by

December. This supernatural confirmation showed me the gravity of this book.

One day as this young man was working on the book, a friend from high school that he hadn't heard from in five years e-mailed him. To make a long story short, they basically start catching up on lost time when my staff member's friend asked him, "Have you ever heard of Jesus appearing to people?" Now, this person did not know that he was working on a book about face-to-face encounters with Jesus because he hadn't mentioned it. Sensing that this was a supernatural confirmation, he held his cool and asked her, "Why would you ask me something like this?" Then the friend replied, "There have been people around me that have come up to me saying, 'Jesus has been appearing to me in dreams and talking to me.'" She mentioned that two to three people had come to her and told her that Jesus had appeared to them in dreams and talked with them.

This young lady was not even saved when she emailed my staff member on December 4, 2008. When the young man in my office told me this, I thought to myself, "What are the odds of this happening right at the time the Lord wants me to get this book out?" I also thought that this would be a good witnessing tool, so I sent her the book! The point is that there is a whole generation of saints and sinners to whom Jesus is appearing. This generation wants to meet the Lord personally, face-to-face, and He is doing that for them. I know that this is how the Lord apprehended me. There is a generation of young and old people who love His face, and they seek it. There are those who are opposed to this and cannot believe that Jesus can do such things, or that He is doing it among His people in this generation. As for this generation of saints, we think we know Jesus because we pray and read the Bible. But our problem is that we tend to impose our own feelings onto the personality of Jesus. It's sort of like when a person becomes hurt or offended after reading an e-mail or a letter, because the words are flat, without expression, and without emotion. We tend to add what we are feeling at the time into what we are reading. But when correct punctuation is added to the letter, the sender's intended emotions and emphasis express their true feelings and message. When Jesus appears to us and we become acquainted with Him, we understand His real personality—only then can we know him. When we go back and read the Bible after meeting Jesus face-to-face, the words have different meaning—we feel the true meaning of the words, and we feel the real personality of Jesus.

There is a hunger in this generation that says, "Don't just tell me about Jesus or God. I want to meet Him personally!" That's what I have attempted to do in this book. You will meet Jesus face-to-face as a result, and He will come to you like He's doing to so many ten thousands of others. By His Spirit, I now write to this generation of those who love His appearances.

The purpose that the Lord gave me for writing this book as your brother in Christ was not to flaunt and pridefully boast of my supernatural experiences with the Lord. This is not my heart, and it's definitely not the Lord's heart or purpose at all. He told me that His purpose for this book was to be a witness of these things which I have seen and heard from Him on a face-to-face level to build faith in your life and to let you know that you too can have this face-to-face relationship with God's Son. It is our loving, Heavenly Father revealing His Son in an intimate way through these face-to-face experiences in this book.

no man knoweth the Son, but the Father; neither knoweth any man the Father, save the Son, and he to whomsoever the Son will reveal Him (Matthew 11:27).

His purpose in this book is to bring you closer to the Son of God in relationship and intimacy by giving you a face-to-face experience with Him that you never dreamed or thought was possible! I say this humbly—I have experienced this and am a witness that you too can have this type of relationship with Jesus on this level. You can have this unprecedented relationship with your Lord and Savior, a relationship like you have never known that will leave you saying as Paul did in Romans, *"O the depths of the riches both of the wisdom and knowledge of God!"* (Rom. 11:33).

In this book, I have included my failures and successes in my relationship with the Lord for the purpose of showing His divinity and my humanity. I am human, and I've made many mistakes in my walk with Jesus. But He has lovingly remained faithful to me in this covenant relationship that we have, through adjusting my heart, mind, and life by dealing with me as a son and correcting me in love. This is what Paul meant when he said he would rather glory in his weaknesses than in his strengths or in himself:

Of such an one will I glory: yet of myself I will not glory, but in mine infirmities. For though I would desire to glory, I shall not be a fool; for I will say the truth: but now I forbear, lest any man should think of me above that which he seeth me to be, or that he heareth of me. And lest I should be exalted [by man] above measure through the abundance of the revelations, there was given to me a thorn in the flesh, the messenger of satan to buffet me, lest I should be exalted above measure....Most gladly therefore will I rather glory in my infirmities (2 Corinthians 12:5-7,9).

Paul knew that by reporting these supernatural experiences that he had with the Lord, these out-of-body trips to Heaven, people would have a tendency to think of him more highly than he really was with God. We are not perfect here on Earth, and all that we will ever be is flesh or earthen vessels until the redemption of our body. We are human and are prone to make mistakes. These experiences can also cause the one who has them to look more perfect than he or she presently is! All of us, even on our best day, are flawed. This doesn't mean that we shouldn't strive to live up to God's best standards by the Holy Ghost. It's not because I have done everything perfect that these experiences with Jesus have been solely granted to me. I can say that I have loved Him to the best of my ability in spite of my faults and failures. All of us have made many mistakes, some greater than others, but nevertheless the Lord loves us and still gives us the opportunity to change and to move on to victory with Him. I have seen by experience that God gets more glory out of our weakest moments than out of our strongest moments (when we live out of our own self accomplishments). This allows His strength to be revealed, and His strength is made perfect or is completely manifested through us in our failures (see 2 Cor. 12:9).

As you learn about the mystery of Jesus Christ, the Son of the Living God, He will begin to appear to you as He's done to many tens of thousands through this message as He promised in His Word. You will begin to meet Him face-to-face in an intimate way when He appears to you! This book has been written to arrange a face-to-face meeting and continual relationship of intimacy between you and God's Son, Jesus—and not only for now in this world, but for all eternity. I love Him, and I love you also, and I really want you to taste what I've experienced with Him as well. This is His heart, and so that makes it my heart and purpose as well. Be blessed as your life experiences the joys of this face-to-face relationship with the presence of Jesus through appearances. Experience what I call with Him, an *Intimacy Beyond Ecstasy.*

CHAPTER 1

The Appearance

The Appearance

The First Face-to-Face Encounter With Jesus

Intimacy Beyond Ecstasy

It was during the Christmas season of December 1989. I fell fast asleep one night, about five to seven days before Christmas Eve. Suddenly, there He was with eyes glowing full of love. Standing in front of me was the man I'd heard about as a little boy my entire life. I had heard about this man from my father and mother, and was taught that He died on the cross for my sins and rose again on the third day from the dead. He still was not truly real to me, only a religious opinion. He was just someone my parents told me about because of their religious beliefs. Then, out of nowhere, He was standing there in front of me, face-to-face. As He stood in front of me, His very presence exuded and emanated such gentleness, a pureness and kindness beyond this world. It was ecstasy! For the first time, I was standing in front of Jesus. My whole being felt Him. You can imagine the ecstasy I felt. It was a feeling of intense glory! It is like wherever He stands He fills the very atmosphere, air, and molecules all around you. Even the atoms inside your very body and being respond to Him. It was total ecstasy—indescribable, blistering with ecstatic eruption! My whole being felt like it was caught up into Heaven. The very atoms in my body made me feel like I was about to explode! Currents of electricity went through me!

He Was All Glorious and Powerful

Standing in front of me was an awesome man—handsome and perfect in stature. He was just a little taller than me, about six feet or more—the perfect height of a normal man. As I gazed upon Him, I saw that the color of His hair was sandy-brownish and parted at the top, coming over the sides of His face, and down His shoulders in waves. The natural words of my vocabulary fail to describe how awesome He was then and how He is presently today! Jesus stood before me with eyes full of love and His face full of light and power. His eyes are so striking that when He looks at you, they penetrate through your very being, character, and nature. When He looks at you with those eyes, He knows everything about you, and nothing is hid from Him. His eyes are like an x-ray or a translucent ray of light. They penetrate and arrest you at the same time. Standing in front of me was Jesus, the King of kings, but He stood there unassuming, just as common as a normal man. I was seeing His humility and meekness, but I didn't understand it then.

It wasn't until years later that I understood what I was seeing in His character which He mentions in Matthew 11:29:

Take My yoke upon you, and learn of Me; for I am meek and lowly in heart.

His humility was so shocking to me. At this point, He was no longer a distant person who sat at the right hand of the throne beside God. He was real! He was alive! He was a man with a personality, and He was standing in front of me!

The One I now love was standing there wearing a beautiful, flowing white robe. There He was, the One I had heard about growing up. He was so powerful, but yet gentle; so merciful, yet full of judgment; so meek and lowly, yet so silently bold. I was captivated by His love. The atmosphere was filled with electricity, but with a peace and serenity beyond articulation. Who was I that the King of kings and the Lord of lords would come and appear to me like this after I had lived such a riotous, worldly, and sinful life? Years later, I wondered about the reason He came like this.

My friend, what and who I am talking about is not just some religious myth, opinion, or fairy tale. He is more real than the very breath of air you've just taken, the clothes you feel on your body, or the book you are holding in your hands reading this very second! I am talking about the most genuine person you will ever want to meet, and I saw Him for the very first time eighteen years ago. He was nothing like the Church has described or portrayed Him to be. Even now, men and women everywhere, and in the Church at large, have failed to describe Him to His fullest.

He Was Suddenly Talking to Me

In this dream, there stood Jesus as I have described. I was standing in front of Him as He was present with me, face-to-face. At the time, I was unaware that years later Exodus 33:11 would become the foundational Scripture that would fuel the passion of my pursuit for His friendship and intimacy.

Exodus 33:11 says,

And the Lord spake unto Moses face-to-face, as a man speaketh unto his friend.

When Jesus looked at me, I knew what He wanted without Him using or moving His mouth. Then He was suddenly talking with me, telling me to come to Him, to give Him my life, and to follow Him. That is all He said to me. His words were not long; they were short. Later I found out why His mouth didn't move. You see, in the Spirit, you don't need the natural faculties of your body to communicate. It is only here on earth that you need them. The Bible says in Romans 8:16, *"The Spirit itself beareth witness with our spirit."* So, when God talks to us, He speaks to our spirit, and we hear Him clearly with our spirit, just as we hear with our natural ears.

He then began to speak saying, *"David, forsake your best friend, give your life to Me, and follow Me."* At that time, my best friend in the world was not saved, nor was he ready to really give his life and heart to the Lord. So Jesus was telling me to forsake that relationship and follow Him. This is what happens with many young people and adults when they initially follow Christ. They are not willing to separate themselves from the world's influence. You can't truly follow Jesus and maintain the worldly relationships or friendships you once had. You must be willing to even give up your best friend if Jesus requires you to!

I know someone is thinking or saying, "but the Bible *says, 'No man hath seen God at any time,'* and, *'no man can see Me, and live'* just as God told Moses" (John 1:18; Exod. 33:20). That's true, but these Scriptures are not referring to Jesus, but to the Father. During the time of Moses, before Jesus shed His blood to put us back into right standing with the Father, no man could see God and live because of sin. Jesus can appear to us, and we can look on His face (see John 1:14). Who did Paul see on the road to Damascus when he was knocked off his horse? Jesus. Who did John the Beloved see on the Isle of Patmos face-to-face? It was Jesus. Jesus also appeared to 500 brethren at one time after His resurrection (see 1 Cor. 15:6). So, don't tell me that this experience wasn't real and that He doesn't appear to men today. He is the same as He was yesterday, today, and forever more. I know it was Jesus the Son of God who was standing in front of me face-to-face.

Forever Changed

After this first experience, little did I know that for the next eighteen years I was about to have incredible, yearly, consistent face-to-face encounters and visitations with Jesus, that would turn into an intimate and personal friendship with Him. These appearances that started as visitations and encounters with Jesus happened through dreams, visions, and in the bright open day while I was wide-awake. An encounter one night in 1989 changed the course of my life forever. Jesus instructed me to write this book, and I have compiled some of the trips to Heaven that I've taken, and the dramatic appearances that my friend Jesus, our risen Lord, has made to me. In agreement with the Word of God, I will share in descriptive detail what I've seen over the years as well as the intimate relationship and friendship that I have developed with Jesus. You can have this personal relationship as well! As you read, I pray that you will be thoroughly blessed as the reality of Jesus the Son of God is channeled through the pages of this book.

But let me also tell you what happened after the first vision I had. It was a few days before Christmas when Jesus first appeared to me in a dream. (I also had another supernatural encounter from God on Christmas Eve, just days after Jesus' first appearance.) It was the night that Santa Claus, for those who play the worldly ritual, was supposed to come. It was the season when schools let students out for Christmas and New Year's break. It was an exciting time for me, but little did I know that the whole course of my life was about to be changed dramatically.

I was seventeen and in the twelfth grade when this all happened to me and my life changed dramatically. Let me back up a little bit and tell you a small portion of who I was before the Lord first appeared to me and saved me.

I was your typical unsaved teenager, smoking dope, marijuana, using bad language and cursing, partying, and having premarital sex. I was even involved with gangs and hung around cocaine-dealing drug lords. I remember one time, before the Lord came to me and saved my life, I was caught in the crossfire of a shoot-out. There were bullets flying everywhere, and I could have possibly been shot and killed. Thank God—He spared my life and protected me! At this time, the Lord sent a young man into my life named Randale Jackson to witness to me. He is one of my best friends today, but I will tell you more about this relationship later.

The Beginning
The Heavens Fill My Room

It all began August 1972, in the small town of Memphis, Tennessee. James H. Taylor and Katie M. Taylor were at the hospital about to give birth to their seventh child. My mother told me she would spend time praying for hours at the church altar when she was pregnant with me in her stomach. Little did they know that the Lord would apprehend that little boy when he turned seventeen, call him to preach the Gospel, and to do Miracle Crusades all over the world!

My mom and dad have nine children. Their firstborn was a boy they named Kenneth. He was followed by Sharon, then Antonio, Angela, Richard (whom I love dearly), Marilyn (my closest sister in age and heart), myself, Zondra, and Christopher (my baby brother). My mother and father were Christians. My father is a minister of the Gospel. God uses him so powerfully as a prophet, and he moves in great power. I've seen newspaper clippings of how God used him to stop a man who held up a bus with a gun. My father walked up to him and said, "I command you to give me the gun in Jesus' name," and the man put the gun in my father's hand! The police couldn't control the situation, but God's power through my father did. They hauled the man off to jail, but my father went with him and led him to Christ. The newspapers and media in Memphis caught this story. This awesome story inspired me; as a young man, I had never heard of God using anyone like this. For many years my parents took us to a beautiful Baptist church. I learned so much there.

We were taken to church every Sunday, and we even had Bible study at home. I always enjoyed it when my mom would sit us down and teach out of the Word of God. I was very inquisitive concerning the supernatural and the various Bible stories. But not even those experiences brought me into the dimension and the realm in God as my first personal encounter with Jesus did. I thank God for my mother and father who brought me up and taught me about the things of God.

I was the seventh child born in the family of nine brothers and sisters. They knew the life I used to live. There was a great transformation and change in my life through the encounter with Jesus that I had at seventeen. Jesus sent a young man named Randale Jackson to witness to me before I had the first visitation from the Lord. Randale and I were members of the same church, Mount Zion Missionary Baptist Church, where C.J. Patterson, whom I love dearly, was pastor. While Randale was away from home at college, he was introduced to Maranatha Ministries in Nashville, Tennessee. Maranatha Ministries was a Spirit-filled ministry unlike the Baptist church that I had been attending. I realize today that God is baptizing a lot of the Baptists with the gift of the Holy Spirit. When Randale was in college, God baptized him with the Holy Spirit. He came back to Memphis witnessing to young people, and God specifically had him key in on me, witnessing to me week after week. He would pick me up, spend time with me, and tell me about Jesus. He was the only young man I saw at the church that was on fire for God. After my conversion, I noticed that there was something different about him. This young man had the baptism of the Holy Spirit, and, like so many others, he was not ashamed of what he had received from God.

Before Jesus first appeared to me, I remember trying to give my life to the Lord because of Randale's witness to me. I remember telling him, "Listen, I have tried to do this, but I keep backsliding and making mistakes over and over again." Then I said, "I did my part, but God did not do His." Oh, how very wrong I was in my thinking! I said, *"I did my part; God did not do His. I am just going to go to hell."* Then he turned to me and said, *"If you want to live right, you need the Holy Spirit."* At that time, I was a Baptist, and I did not know who the Holy Spirit was. The only thing I knew about the Holy Ghost was that the pastor would baptize someone and say, *"I baptize you in the name of the Father, the Son, and the Holy Ghost."* That was it! Two years later I would be introduced not just to the baptism of the Holy Spirit but to the person of the Holy Spirit (by a great man of God named Benny Hinn), which I will also tell you about later in this book.

The Supernatural Heavens Invade My Room

It was about 11:00 P.M., and I was at home on a wintry Christmas Eve night in 1989. My light was the only one on in the house. I got down on my knees, looked up to Heaven, and said, *"Lord, You came to me in a dream, and You showed me that you are real."* Then I paused, thinking—*was it just a dream, or was He really real?* Was He really alive as I saw Him days earlier?" Then I continued and said, *"If You are truly real, manifest Yourself to me more."* I did not know what I was asking for! I was just repeating what Randale had told me a few days earlier. I continued, *"And give me the Holy Spirit that I may live right."* After I said those words, I suddenly heard the voice of God audibly in my room the same way you would hear an announcer over the radio or someone standing in front of you talking. I heard His voice clearly, and it shook the room. God Almighty was speaking to me. He said, *"Speak in tongues!"* Now, you have to understand that I knew nothing about the Holy Spirit, tongues, or the gifts of the Holy Spirit. The only thing I knew was that the Holy Spirit was the third person in the Trinity.

I did not know what speaking in tongues was, nor did I understand what He was asking of me. I was only baptized in water and hadn't been taught about this yet. I knew that everyone else in the house was asleep. He spoke audibly again and said, *"Speak in tongues."* After He said it the second time, I parted my mouth to ask Him what tongues were and what He was asking me to do. As I parted my lips, a language came out of me that I had never heard. I began to talk to Him in a language that I did not understand. A few seconds went by before it stopped, and I didn't know what happened. Intense glory filled my room, and I thought I was going crazy. You have to understand that I grew up in the Baptist church and did not know anything about the Holy Ghost; I had never heard a message on tongues or the in-filling of the Holy Spirit.

Baptized With the Holy Spirit

This marked the beginning of a revolution in my life. Every moment of my life was given to relationship and intimacy with Jesus, the One I had seen five days prior in the dream. I was praying, reading the Word, and seeking God intensely. I knew that after I had seen Jesus, He was truly alive, and that also meant everything else in the Bible was true. I said to myself, "Since Jesus has risen from the dead, and I have seen Him, then everything else is true." I wanted all of it! I went after Him. The more I sought Him, the more He would come and appear to me at various times and intervals. All I knew is that He was coming to me personally and on a consistent basis.

Without exaggeration, my room was engulfed with the atmosphere of Heaven and a cloudy mist. My room was literally lifted to the atmosphere of Heaven. My room did not actually have a door, so I had to put a bed sheet at the entryway. Often, before I put the bed sheet up every single day, a glistening angel with a sword would be standing at the door of my room. It was like I was not even at home. My mom was worried about me because I stayed in my room for hours and days at a time. I would come out and fellowship with the family at times, but I was caught up experiencing heavenly things in my room. My room was literally filled with celestial air or an electrical atmosphere.

I remember one time I was so hungry for God that I intensely read the Word all day and did not come out of my room. As I was reading, I was caught up in the glorious presence of God again and began fellowshiping and opening my heart to Him. I would tell Him how much I loved Him and wanted to know Him. I continued reading the Word until I was very sleepy and dozing off. I shook myself to wake up because I wanted to keep reading. I heard His voice say, *"Go to sleep now."* Then, Psalm 127:2 came to me, *"He giveth His beloved sleep."* I replied, *"Lord, just a few more minutes,"* and I stayed up reading a little bit more. My Bible was open in my hands when I heard the Lord say again: *"Go to sleep now."* I still did not go to sleep because I wanted a little bit more time. As I sat with my eyes fully opened and the Bible in my hands, it suddenly shut by itself. It closed as if I had taken my hands and closed it, but one of my hands was still flat. God shut the Bible and said, *"I said, go to sleep now."* The Bible records this type of experience in Scripture: *"...and much study is a weariness of the flesh"* (Eccles. 12:12). This supernatural experience of the Bible shutting in my hands, in front of my eyes, happened twice during the first year of my conversion.

I began to search the Scriptures day after day, and then I ran across the second chapter of Acts where they spoke in tongues. I jumped up and exclaimed, *"That's what happened to me!"* Suddenly, I saw my life in the pages of the Bible. This is what I want you to understand. I didn't know about speaking in tongues. So, when I read it in the Bible it was like a new revelation to me. Suddenly, Jesus and the baptism of the Holy Spirit came in my life by revelation. It was ecstasy!

The Communion and Fellowship of the Holy Spirit

*The grace of the Lord Jesus Christ, and the love of God, **and the communion of the Holy Ghost**, be with you all. Amen* (2 Corinthians 13:14).

*If there be therefore any consolation in Christ, if any comfort of love, **if any fellowship of the Spirit**...* (Philippians 2:1).

As I've stated earlier, I was filled and baptized with the Holy Spirit at my conversion, but I knew nothing about the Holy Spirit as a person. The Lord began teaching me about the wonderful person of the Holy Ghost through the ministry of Benny

Hinn. Before then, I had only viewed the Holy Spirit as a gift from God and knew that He gave us gifts, mainly to speak with other tongues. How sad it is that the Church has treated someone as awesome as He is this way.

THE HOLY SPIRIT IS THE ONE WHO GLORIFIES THE PERSON JESUS.

Well, the revelation that Benny gave in his book *Good Morning, Holy Spirit* concerning the communion, fellowship, and person of the Holy Spirit changed my life and broke this religious mindset or background that I was taught about the Holy Spirit. The Holy Spirit became more of a person just as Jesus was to me.[1] After Benny pointed out in his book that, according to Scripture, Jesus referred to the Holy Spirit as "He" and not "it" (as the Holy Spirit had been presented to me in my church background), I saw that He was a person and not a "thing."

> *And when He is come, He will reprove the world of sin....Howbeit when He, the Spirit of truth, is come, He will guide you into all truth: for He shall not speak of Himself; but whatsoever He shall hear, that shall He speak; and He will shew you things to come* (John 16:8,13).

As I read the first three pages of this book, I was so stirred with a hunger for the person and communion of the Holy Spirit that I put the book down and immediately went into my closet on a three-day fast. The first three pages of this book inspired me so much that I had to put it down and seek the Lord. After the three-day fast, I picked the book back up and finished reading. From this time in 1993 when I was introduced to the person of the Holy Spirit, my spiritual life and relationship with Jesus took off to a whole different dimension. My prayer time and witness about Jesus took on power! Every day I fellowshiped and communed with the Holy Spirit, and something erupted inside of me. I thank God for Benny Hinn. He has been a great blessing to the Body. God worked through Benny Hinn's life to show me the person of the Holy Spirit, who in turn introduced me to the real Jesus.

Face-To-Face Visitations From Jesus Increased After I Was Introduced to the Person of the Holy Spirit

At this point, my relationship with the Lord began to increase. Jesus became more real to me. It's because the Holy Spirit is the One who makes Jesus real. Jesus promised us that the Holy Spirit would glorify Him. He said,

He shall glorify Me (John 16:14).

That's why I believe that the Lord was introducing the Holy Spirit to the Body of Christ in the early '90s in a new way—as a person. Now the next level is the person of the Holy Spirit revealing and glorifying who Jesus is as a person. After this, Jesus will reveal who the Father is to us. The Lord has ordained the writing of this book by the Holy Spirit with the purpose of making real and glorifying the Person of Jesus Christ. Jesus is a very real person, and God and His Holy Spirit want you to know the Son of God face-to-face!

Full Speed Ahead With Intensity

I began to seek God intensely because I knew there was more to Him than what I had seen in church. I started to spend hundreds of hours with the Lord. As a young person, I stopped being interested in your normal teenage activities such as sports and going to the mall. I was so hungry for God and wanted more of what I had experienced with Jesus that I stopped watching television completely. I didn't have to force myself to do this. It was the Lord's captivating love that inspired me to be close to Him in this way. It was not a chore, a job, or a burden for me to do this. It was a delight! At this time, I spent countless of hours on my knees praying, crying, bubbling over with joy on the inside, laughing, and fellowshiping intimately with the Lord.

I read Daniel's life in the Bible and how he prayed three times a day, so I made a pattern to do the same before school, after school, and at night before bed (see Dan. 6:10). I also remember the times when I would come home from school exhausted. Now, at this point I was still in the twelfth grade, so after Christmas break, I went back to school telling everyone that I had seen Jesus. I became a witness from that day forward. My friends that I was in a gang with knew me before this experience. So when they saw this drastic change over the holiday they knew it was real.

I told everyone that I came in contact with about Jesus, including my teachers, and led as many as I could to the Lord at school. Every day I came home from school, and I would rush to get back into fellowship with Jesus in that glorious atmosphere of Heaven in my room. Every day I would see the angel standing at my door with a sword. I prayed three times a day before school, after school at 5:00 P.M. (which was a special, specified time to meet the Lord), and at night before bed. So sometimes I was so exhausted that I would go to sleep before this special time of fellowship with the Lord.

I would get home from school around 3:00 or 3:30 P.M. so I could get some rest because I was looking forward to the Lord meeting with me. There was a great excitement because supernatural things would always happen in my room during prayer time. I became faithful in this routine, and it never failed that, after coming home exhausted from school and falling asleep, I was awakened by someone pulling and raising one of my legs clear up in the air off my bed. (Now I said "Someone" because when I would wake up I did not see anyone, not even the angel that would stand at my door during prayer times, but I knew it was the Lord.) When I would wake up after this experience, the clock in my room would display 4:55 P.M. It never failed. This would happen frequently when I came home from school tired and would fall asleep. I understood that it was the Lord keeping covenant with the time I had set to meet with Him. I'll never forget the day my father said out of the clear blue sky, *"David, whenever you set a prayer time to meet the Lord, He holds you to that time, and He will meet you there before you get there."*

I was amazed because I had never mentioned anything to him. I thought to myself at that time, *"That's why I am being awakened at 4:55 P.M. every day because He wants me to meet Him on time.*" I have also heard of Christians who have had a similar experience of God waking them up three nights in a row at the same time each night. It couldn't be a coincidence. It's God! If this is happening to you or has ever happened to you, God is trying to fellowship with you for some purpose that you will not find out unless you get up at that time and pray. What an experience! I've never forgotten it to this day!

The Intimacy Continues; The Ecstasy Begins
Jesus Takes Me to the Waterfall

Even after high school when I went off to college to become a chef, the hunger didn't die. As a matter of fact, my hunger and the visitations grew greater in intensity. These were the times when I learned the most, and Jesus would come to personally teach me and give me answers. As this happened, the Lord and I became closer. The more I sought Him and drew near to Him, the more He drew near to me, and we became friends. I say this not out of presumption but out of proof from the Lord Himself who validated our friendship with signs and wonders. For instance, one sign occurred while I was doing my college internship. I was sent to Rhode Island where there are a lot of young people serving satan and the occult. I remember during that time of my internship, the Lord had me witnessing and getting a lot of people saved and delivered from the occult. Now battling witchcraft has a way of affecting and wearing down your mind. I became so extremely tired from battle and needed a break.

I remember talking to one of my college friends, Richard Lambert, saying, *"I really would like to go to a waterfall to get away, meditate, and spend some deep time with the Lord."* I have always liked going to waterfall settings to meditate on the Lord, but at this time

I didn't have any transportation to go anywhere. It was barely two days later that the Lord came and got me; this time it wasn't just a dream. He came and got me in body and took me to a waterfall that was so beautiful. It had three tiers of water flowing so beautifully. I knew this wasn't Heaven because we never left earth's atmosphere.

The Waterfall Experience

"One of the Greatest Moments of My Life With Him"

And the Lord said, Behold, there is a place by Me, and thou shalt stand upon a rock: And it shall come to pass, while My glory passeth by, that I will put thee in a clift of the rock (Exodus 33:21-22).

He took me at a fast rate, and we appeared on the cliff's ledge facing the opposite side of the waterfall. I remember standing on the edge of this high mountain next to Jesus looking over across at another high mountain from which this waterfall towered down. It was a rocky cliff that I remembered my feet touching. We stood and looked at this beautiful water falling off the cliff. To this day, I don't know where in the world the Lord took me, and I didn't even think to ask. I was just caught up in the moment being with the Lord again. My eyes are welling up with tears while I am writing this to you as if I was still there now. I remember it with such vivid memory. Oh, how I love Him! There He was again. Jesus had on, as usual, a beautiful, white robe that came down to His feet. He stood by me quietly while we watched the water. I could tell by the expression on Jesus' face that He enjoyed looking at this waterfall just as much as I did. I didn't know that He liked water and looking at waterfalls also, but years later I would come to find out that He has His own personal waterfall in His backyard at His mansion in Heaven which I will tell you of later. I remember standing on the right side of Him. As He stood next to me, He said nothing at this point. We just fellowshiped. One thing that I learned about Jesus is that He does not talk very much. He is a man of few words. Sometimes words are unexpressive and can destroy a beautiful moment.

He Stood Side by Side With Me Like a Friend

*And the night following the **Lord stood by Him*** (Acts 23:11).

*And the Lord descended in the cloud, **and stood with him there*** (Exodus 34:5).

*The **Lord stood with me**, and strengthened me* (2 Timothy 4:17).

I also learned to follow Jesus' lead. For instance, if He is quiet, then I am quiet, or if He gives me an opportunity to speak, then I speak. I just follow what He does when He visits. So I was quiet at the waterfall as well while He stood there until He allowed the opportunity for me to speak. Because the water was so beautiful, I said, "Lord, can I get up under the water and splash in it?" His gentle reply was, *"No."* Then He went on to say, *"If you would get up under the water, it would kill you because of the weight and tons of water coming off of the cleft."* During that time, I couldn't tell if He had taken me in my physical body form until He answered my question. It felt like one of the other visitations in a dream where He would come and take my spirit out of my body. Now, I understand clearly when Paul said in Second Corinthians 12:2-3, *"Whether in the body, I cannot tell; or whether out of the body, I cannot tell."* When Jesus said this to me, it dawned on me that I wasn't there in spirit only, because if I was, the water would have passed right through me without hurting me.

He was, in so many words, telling me that it could kill me because I was there with Him in body. There are times when Jesus can come and take your spirit out of your body, and then there are times He can come and translate you in physical body form. When the Lord takes your spirit out of your body, your spirit man looks just like the image of your natural man so you can't really tell the difference unless there is a distinction made as in this case. I just thought about seeing waterfalls in my mind, mentioned the idea to my friend, and Jesus did this for me without me even asking. At that time, I began to understand what the Scripture means when it says, *"Now unto Him that is able to do exceeding abundantly above all we ask or think"* (Eph. 3:20).

After this experience, I began to realize that we had developed something special. It was a deep fellowship and communion. It was ecstasy; no, it was an intimacy beyond ecstasy, but I didn't know that it could get any more intense! This was not even the ultimate experience. I didn't know it, but He was about to challenge me to receive the ultimate compliment and reward from Himself—to become His personal friend. I didn't know it, but the relationship was about to go to another dimension. It wasn't until years later that I realized what had really taken place.

HE ACTUALLY CALLED ME HIS FRIEND.

The Encounters Turn Into an Intimate Relationship Beyond Ecstasy

Another way that this friendship was revealed to me was through His command to leave my parents' house, to give up my career as a chef, to give up everything, and to follow Him wherever He sent me. The Lord had instructed me to walk by faith without anything (not even money) and to go to a city on nothing. My parents didn't understand at this time, but this was the price that the Lord told me I had to pay at the age of 19 to follow His destiny for my life. The Lord spoke supernaturally to a pastor that I did not know to receive me into his home. This pastor was a kind man from the Caribbean Islands, and at that time I was young and imma-ture in multi-cultural ministry. I remember him getting of-fended because I laid down in the bed with my shoes on, and this was disrespectful to him. I didn't know that this, and other things like it, offended him culturally. As a result, he didn't get to know me, and he began spreading evil things against me because he didn't understand some of my manner-isms. (I admit to this day that I did act quite strange, but God has taught me balance.)

Well, a little time passed by as he kept speaking these evil things until one night when Jesus came to him in a dream and said to him, *"David is My friend, and I have sent him here. Now, you will be dumb and unable to talk for speaking against him until you repent."* This pastor woke up out of the dream dumb. He could not talk physically for a number of days. After he had de-cided to repent, he came to me broken, and his mouth was loosed. That's when he told me all that I've just told you. I had wondered

39

what was wrong with him when he was walking around the house for days without speaking to me. I thought that maybe he was fasting or maybe offended by something. When he told me this, I then understood. He started having a different mindset toward me from that day forward. The Scripture records that the Lord rebuked kings for Abraham's sake. The Scripture also shares how God rebuked men in dreams for mistreating people as in the case of Jacob's father-in-law Laban:

> *And God came to Laban the Syrian in a dream by night, and said unto him, Take heed that thou speak not to Jacob either good or bad....* ***It is in the power of my hand to do you hurt:*** *but the God of your father spake unto me yesternight, saying, Take thou heed that thou speak not to Jacob either good or bad....Except the God of my father, the God of Abraham, and the fear of Isaac, had been with me, surely thou hadst sent me away now empty. God hath seen mine affliction and the labour of my hands,* ***and rebuked thee yesternight*** (Genesis 31:24,29,42).

When these things began to happen again, I knew that the Lord and I had something special even though I didn't understand how. This shocked me because I didn't know we were that close until Jesus spoke of it and allowed this mighty demonstration to take place by the witness of another man's testimony. Jesus called me His friend at this time in 1992 when I was only 19 years old. Again, I did not understand this. I had only been saved for two-and-a-half years. According to my religious mind-set, this established friendship between us happened so quickly according to my standards, but I knew the Lord could not lie. I thought, *"Is this all I have to do?"*

These manifestations started taking place from these sovereign acts of the Lord without my control or knowledge, and He allowed me to see our friendship through these face-to-face experiences that I had and that this pastor had when the Lord defended our friendship to him. Every one of you reading this book can also have the same face-to-face experience and friendship with Jesus that I've just shared with you.

YOU CAN SEE JESUS.

You Can Have This Relationship Too

You can have this continual face-to-face contact with Jesus through appearances. This is not just a onetime supernatural encounter or a sign-and-wonder experience with the Lord that I'm talking about. That is shallow! It's great but shallow; I'm talking about a face-to-face relationship of intimacy and friendship that you can have with the Lord continually for the rest of your life. Jesus shed His blood for you to have this level of relationship with Him. You can have the greatest relationship with the Lord ever known to man yet! You may ask, *"What did you do to get that relationship with Jesus?"* Some would say, *"You don't have to do anything;, it's just by grace and mercy."* There is a balance. I believe everything God allows is by His mercy and grace, but at the same time there are things He requires us to do before He will act upon it. Jesus said, "Draw nigh unto Me" and then He says, "and I will draw nigh unto you" (see James 4:8).

In my three-year college experience, I spent countless hours on that cold bathroom floor in my room. I would sing and worship the Lord for hours. I wouldn't make it the focus to ask for His gifts, power, or ministry, but I would sing and ask for a deep closer walk, relationship, and friendship with Him. There are hundreds of more visitations and appearances Jesus gave me that I could tell you. But these recorded throughout this whole book were written so that you might develop a greater hunger for this special face-to-face relationship with Jesus and to also show you that you can have the same. If you do not want a real face-to-face appearance and relationship with the Lord Jesus Christ on this level, you might as well close the contents of this book forever! Because after reading this, you will have an encounter and an appearance from the Lord like you have never experienced that will change your life forever! Then after the initial appearance encounter that the Lord will give you, you will begin to have a consistent face-to-face relationship in this way with the Lord. I can't say how often, frequent, or even the amount of time that He will spend visiting you. All I know is suddenly, when you least expect it, He will show up and change your life forever.

ASK THE LORD FOR THIS RELATIONSHIP NOW.

I know that there are those who may be reading this book who haven't given their life to Jesus. He loves you too and wants to give you this same experience just as He did for me when I was unsaved at seventeen. I want you right now to do what I did in 1989 when I was just a teenager. Lift one of your hands up to

God while this book is in your other hand now and say these words, *"Lord Jesus, I give You my life. I confess that You are Lord and that God Your Father has raised You from the dead. I believe in You and Your finished work that You did for me on Calvary. I receive Your blood that You shed for me, and I ask You to forgive me for every evil sin that I've done against You up until now. You are Lord in my life, and I ask You to give me Your precious Holy Spirit that I may live the way that You want me to live. Baptize me now in the Holy Spirit and bring me now in this face-to-face fellowship and relationship with Jesus so I can experience the tangibleness of how real He is. Father, I ask this in Jesus' name. Amen."*

I began to seek the Lord asking Him about the reality of Christ in the Church. The more I sought the Lord, the more He showed me how we are supposed to be moving with a greater level of glory and power than the early church did in Acts or the prophets and apostles did in the Old Testament. I did not see this happening, and I began to get even more frustrated. I sought God continually, fasted almost every single day, and I saw Him give me answers. I will share some of these answers with you in the pages of this book. During my college days, about two to three full years, I had spent countless hours with the Lord in fellowship. I sat on that cold bathroom floor singing the same song for hours wanting to be close to Him, and I stayed in my college dorm for days. In college I loved Him so much that, when the Lord commanded, I stayed in the dorm during the Thanksgiving and Christmas holiday breaks to spend extra time with Him when other students went home to see their families.

He Promised That He Will Come to You

During a visitation, Jesus promised me that He would draw closer to everyone who picks up this book and reads it. By the time that you complete this book, you will not only have developed a greater hunger, but you will also gain the relationship that you have desired to have with Him. You will gain beyond what your wildest imagination has dreamed of in your relationship with Him. So, be ready for your life to be dramatically revolutionized and turned upside down as you read and discover what has been waiting for you in this face-to-face relationship. Since the world began, God has had a plan for your life. Learn like thousands of others how you can experience a face-to-face relationship with Jesus—one in which He appears to you not only once, but on a regular basis. The Lord also promised me, saying, *"Those who read this book will begin to have visitations and appearances from Me personally, David."* Jesus promised me that what He has already made happen in my life will begin to fall on you, but in an even greater measure.

He said, *"Even those to whom I have already appeared, or who are having appearance experiences, will see a dramatic increase and will have many more encounters!"* Get ready! We have already begun to hear testimonies from a number of people who have heard my testimony and started having face-to-face experiences with God. This started with me personally at home and then spread to pastors and their wives, and even to their church members. This started happening in churches of every size. This has even started happening to pastors who have 400 churches under their leadership! Jesus is appearing to them and establishing friendships and deep intimacy resulting in covenant relationships. Their testimonies have caused revival to break out in different regions. So, do you really want to know Jesus in a way you have not known Him yet? I don't just mean to know Christ or have the knowledge of Christ, but to have the highest and most excellent knowledge of Christ. Don't you want more than going to church just to hear about Him or maybe to feel His presence or anointing power!? Don't you want more? Did you know there was more? Most people don't.

Don't Be Afraid
You Do Not Have to Be Afraid of the Lord Appearing to You.

To some, this may sound exciting for Jesus to appear to you face-to-face, but at the same time fearful to others for the simple reason that they would be seeing the Lord. This behavior or fear is not unusual. When the Lord or His angel appeared to most people who are recorded in history, He had to tell them to *"Fear not"* while He was standing in front of them (see Gen. 15:1)! This is His same admonition to you when He comes. Don't be afraid. There is nothing to fear in the bad sense of this word. Although great reverence is manifested from the intensity of His presence, He does not want us to fear Him in an ungodly way or in a fleshly manner. It's just the opposite. He wants us to love Him and experience Him! He wants us to have confidence when He appears to us (see 1 John 2:28). Every time that the Lord has visited a person, He immediately encouraged them against fear. He wants us to have confidence at His coming and not to be ashamed or afraid!

Life Is Pointless Without This

I pray that you will be thoroughly blessed by the contents of this book. It is my highest desire that you will fulfill the call of God on your life and inherit the awesome glory and riches that belong to you by finding and winning a friendship with the Lord in this face-to-face way. It is your destiny to know Him. He is your exceedingly great reward and prize. Life is pointless without this! Life has no meaning without Him. Do you know what I am talking about? Your ministry purpose, calling, and His assignment for your life are not your destiny. He is your destiny! He is your prize!

Some may be asking, *"Where in the Bible does He promise to do this—or even say that He wants to do this in our lives as Christians?"* You may be saying now, *"I've never heard of such a thing as this, that I can have a literal face-to-face relationship with the Lord, one in which He will come to me by appearing to me face-to-face."* Some may be saying, *"All I've heard quoted is 'blessed is he that believes and has not seen.'"* *"What does seeing Him have to do with my walk or intimacy with Him?"* *"Why do I have to see Him?"* And, *"If He does want us to see Him, why?"* *"What are the benefits of this?"* *"How will this affect my life?"* I will answer all of these questions according to the Word of God, and show you how this is possible and where Jesus' promise is found in Scripture. So read on, beloved. Without question, you will certainly be changed when these awesome visitation appearances from Jesus begin in your life. He is on His way, and He's surely coming to visit and appear to you as He promised in His Word.

ENDNOTE

1. Benny Hinn, *Good Morning, Holy Spirit* (Nashville, TN: Thomas Nelson, Inc., 2004).

He Promised in His Word to Come to You

The Opportunity of a Lifetime

He Promised in His Word to Come to You

His Covenant With Us of Appearances

JESUS PROMISED IN SCRIPTURE TO APPEAR TO YOU.

*He that hath My commandments, and keepeth them, he it is that loveth Me: and he that loveth Me shall be loved of My Father, and **I will love him, and will manifest Myself to him*** (John 14:21).

In this passage of Scripture, Jesus makes His covenant to *"manifest"* Himself plainly to the reader. This is shown when Jesus says, *"I will love him and will manifest Myself to him."* This word *manifest* in this context comes from the Greek word *emphanizo* which means, "To appear to or show one's self in person." It also means, "To exhibit in person or to disclose oneself by words."[1] This is awesome, and it was in Scripture all this time before I ever knew or understood what was going on in my life! Jesus was appearing to me, but I didn't understand all of this until years later when He showed me according to Scripture. Another thing to note is that this manifestation of the Lord doesn't necessarily constitute Him appearing where we see Him face-to-face. An appearance can take place when He discloses Himself in words to you. In other words, you may be asleep in a dream, or awake, and you don't see Him, but you hear a voice (His voice) talking to you audibly. This was also called an appearance from the Lord. We see this manifested more in the Old Testament like when He appeared to Moses and disclosed Himself to him by words. Moses didn't literally see the face of God at the burning bush or in the cloud, but he heard the voice of the Lord speaking out of the cloud. This is an appearance from the Lord—when He manifests Himself to you in the form of words. Paul had this same experience on the road to Damascus when Jesus appeared to him in the physical realm. A bright light from the Lord's presence became so brilliant that it knocked him down on the ground as he heard His voice speaking words. It was the voice of Jesus. This is the same thing that the Lord does to us sometimes when we are in deep sleep and we hear a voice speaking words to us. This is an appearance but not a face-to-face appearance from the Lord. This type of appearance is known as the Lord manifesting Himself to us by the words of His voice.

It's Still an Appearance

HE'S STILL THERE EVEN THOUGH YOU
ONLY HEAR HIS *VOICE*.

Disclosure by Words

As I've mentioned, when Jesus promises to *"manifest"* Himself to us by visibly appearing, this also means He does this by disclosing or revealing Himself by the words of His voice. In the Old Testament, when it mentions the Lord appearing to different ones, you will find that most of the time the Lord's appearance was not a face-to-face appearance. Instead, they were only allowed to hear His voice as He stood next to them, without them seeing that He was there. The Lord stood with Samuel when He spoke to him by a voice. The Bible called it an appearance from the Lord.

And the Lord appeared again in Shiloh: for the Lord revealed Himself to Samuel in Shiloh by the word of the Lord (1 Samuel 3:21).

And the Lord came, and stood, and called as at other times, Samuel, Samuel. Then Samuel answered, Speak; for Thy servant heareth (1 Samuel 3:10).

So when it says the Lord stood with Samuel as at other times, these were actual visitations and appearances where the Lord was standing right there by him, but only allowing His voice audibly to be heard and not necessarily His face or body to be seen! You see, after the Fall, Jehovah God the Father couldn't disclose His raw face to us, but instead when He would physically come to the earth (as in the case with Adam), the Bible records that His voice was heard as He would come walking in the cool of the day. We know that a voice does not walk.

And they heard the voice of the Lord God walking in the garden in the cool of the day: and Adam and his wife hid themselves from the presence of the Lord God amongst the trees of the garden (Genesis 3:8).

What this meant is that the Lord was actually there in person, but could only disclose Himself to Adam and Eve by the words of His voice because of their sin. These were tragic words because the Lord could reveal Himself by face and not just by voice before Adam and Eve had sinned. So when you actually hear the voice of the Lord speaking to you while you are in deep sleep or awake, that's a visitation of the Lord really standing there in person with you even though you do not see Him. This is still awesome! Don't take it lightly. But I don't want you to be distracted by these types of appearances from Lord in which He only discloses His voice to you. In this book I am talking about a more advanced New Testament face-to-face appearance from Jesus. It's when He reveals His face to you! David wasn't content with the Lord just disclosing His appearance to him by words. The Bible mentions that the Lord would speak to him in a vision by words.

Then Thou spakest in vision to Thy holy one, and saidst, I have laid help upon one that is mighty; I have exalted one chosen out of the people (Psalm 89:19).

*Then Solomon began to build the house of the Lord at Jerusalem in mount Moriah, **where the Lord appeared unto David his father**, in the place that David had prepared in the threshingfloor of Ornan the Jebusite* (2 Chronicles 3:1).

The Bible also records that the Lord appeared to King David and that he had a face-to-face relationship with the Lord. As I've said earlier, when the Bible speaks of the Lord having a face-to-face relationship with men in the Old Testament, it isn't referring to a literal, visible appearance from God's face, although He was very present in front of them at the time. Today we can have a face-to-face relationship with Jesus, God's Son, one in which He will visibly manifest and show His face to us.

The Opportunity of a Lifetime

Understanding That He Wants to Manifest Himself to You by Appearances

It is important to realize in entirety what Jesus is saying here. There are so many people who don't believe this message of intimacy—that Jesus wants this intimate love relationship with them face-to-face by appearing in person to them. Some, as I have heard, who have been Christians for many years, go their whole walk with God without realizing that this face-to-face level with Jesus is even possible. They have never experienced Him in a face-to-face way. I declare unto you Jesus' words, by my own experience, that He will manifest Himself to you.

He's done this with so many others in biblical times and in our day today. The Scripture records Jesus demonstrating His desire and nature to appear to us. He appeared to Mary Magdalene and to the other Mary after His resurrection (see Matt. 28:9). He appeared to the apostles and to five hundred men at one time. He also appeared to Paul who gives an account in First Corinthians 15:4-8 that the Lord appeared to Him and others. This is seen in his statement when he says, *"And last of all He was seen of me."* You have to also understand that all of these appearances from Jesus to men were post-resurrection. The Lord has been appearing to man throughout years and centuries. This is not a new thing that He started doing in our time. It's new to us!

THE FACE-TO-FACE LOVE COVENANT REVEALED.

He Just Wants Us to Love Him

Another point in this context is that Jesus says there's a requirement of love for Him to do this in our lives: *"We love Him by keeping His commandments"* (see John 14:21). We show Him we love Him by keeping His commandments. We must be loyal to His commandments by keeping them. Now, don't get confused here; Jesus is not saying that we have to basically keep all of His commands by being perfect. If that's what it meant, then all of us are disqualified from this level of relationship with Him. Those in and out the Bible, myself included, would never have experienced this relationship through appearances that I am now talking to you about. This word *keep* means to guard, watch over, defend, cherish, and keep in one's memory to perform the duties told even after one has failed to do so.[2] This is the personal love covenant relationship that He's made available between Himself and each individual personally. It's all about loving Him. I call this ongoing face-to-face manifestation of the Lord in my life a "love covenant" since it's based on Love! All of this is the basis of a covenant of love with Jesus. Jesus is interested in being loved by you in a special way! He wants your love. Love is not predicated upon always being perfect or doing everything right. Your love for Him can increase even as a result of having to be forgiven for your sins, mistakes, and failures. Jesus said that those who have been forgiven much, love much (see Luke 7:47).

You also must understand in this context of Scripture that He is not talking about a onetime appearance, but an ongoing relationship where He appears face-to-face to those who love him

He Wants to Know You Face-to-Face

And there arose not a prophet since in Israel like unto Moses, whom the Lord knew face to face (Deuteronomy 34:10).

but then face to face: now I know in part; but then shall I know even as also I am known (1 Corinthians 13:12).

This is a fellowship that He's speaking about where He continually comes back again and again and appears to you. Jesus also said in the verses before this in John 14:18: *"I will not leave you comfortless: I will come to you."* In this context, He wasn't just referring to the Holy Spirit being the only comforter; He was also referring to Himself comforting us by coming personally! You notice, He never said He would just come one time or a limited number of times. He left it open. He said, *"I will love him, and I will manifest Myself to him"* (see John 14:21). There is a balance. Jesus has not made this command, *"to love Him"* as a law for Him to appear to us. This is demonstrated to us when the Lord appeared to Paul even after he murdered Christians! There was no love involved on Paul's part, but it was a sovereign act of God's grace and love. It also was a sovereign act of kindness for God to send Jesus to earth over 2000 years ago, who manifested in the flesh and appeared openly. In this context, He's talking to those who want this ongoing face-to-face relationship, one in which He will manifest Himself by appearing to us through the conditions of loving Him by keeping His commandments.

The word *face* first appears in the Book of Genesis and it comes from the Hebrew word *paniym* which means "the countenance" or the "front side" of something.[3] It also means the surface or the visible side of something or someone, of persons, God, water, and the list goes on. In this book, we are talking about having a face-to-face relationship with Jesus, one in which you can visibly see the front side of His countenance. This is special. Do you want this? What if I told you that Jesus wanted you to have this level of relationship with Him! What if I showed you according to Scripture Jesus saying that He wanted to do this in your life? Would you believe it and accept it? Well, my friends, it is real, and Jesus did express and say that He would do this in the lives of His people. Do you want this with Him? It is the most intimate way one can express oneself.

Speaking with someone face-to-face is the perfect expression of friendship, love, and intimacy with a friend, spouse, children, or anyone else you love. When you cannot show your face in a relationship with a person, something is wrong. Well, Jesus understands this, and that's just one of the reasons why He comes to you face-to-face in this way. Being face-to-face with God represents intimacy and an expression of love that surpasses talking on the telephone (prayer) and just hearing responses on the other end of the line.

It's beyond just feeling His presence or sensing He's there. These are still wonderful, but vague, experiences with the Lord. Most Christians are just content with feeling the Lord's presence in a room, in a service, or in their prayer time! There's more!!! Yes, much more! And I've experienced it and am continually experiencing Him in this way consistently every year. But even still, I want so much more! I'm not content with a onetime experience or all the ones I have had until now! I still want more from the Lord! This is not a onetime experience but a lifetime adventure of intimacy with the Lord face-to-face!

PURSUE HIS *APPEARANCE*.

How would you feel if you had just met someone that you didn't know and you talked on the phone for hours, days, weeks, and months until a whole year had passed by? This generation is so accustomed to this type of relationship with e-mail and internet chatting. We can meet someone, talk to them for a whole year, and never meet them face-to-face. That's dangerous! It's not until you meet a person face-to-face that you will learn what their values are and who they really are! The face reveals the character of the person. You learn volumes about a person you have just met when you go out with them and sit down face-to-face. This is where the Church is presently. They are content with the experience of feeling the Lord's presence, fascinated with talking to Him in prayer, and getting a response back from His voice. But I'm not! And there is a whole generation out there that's not content with just this limited relationship with the Lord. God wants to do something new and fresh that will blow your mind off the charts of where you have ever been with Him, or where religious traditions and heretics have limited God!

He is alive, and He is a Person. He will be a friend to you! Even *now!* Just ask today. Today is your day to experience this awesome relationship and a level of intimacy you have never had with the Lord.

He Promises to Come to You

I will come to you (John 14:18).

When I say to you that Jesus is going to personally come to you, I'm not just making this up, and neither am I going solely on the fact that Jesus personally told me to tell you that He would. The Word of God is the foundation I stand on concerning this! Jesus told me that He would appear to those of you who are reading this book face-to-face. Isn't that awesome? You ought to be excited! Since I've been preaching this message of face-to-face intimacy, thousands have begun to experience this type of relationship with Jesus as a result of our ministry.

My children had face-to-face visits from the Lord when they were only seven and nine years old. I asked the Lord to visit my children because I know how impacting it is for them to have an experience from the Lord on their own beyond the influence of their parents teaching them about Jesus. When Jesus first appeared to me at seventeen years of age, this had a great impact on my life beyond what my parents had taught me. Your children and your whole family can experience this as well. Even the families in the staff of our worldwide ministry have had appearances from the Lord Jesus Christ. It's happening everywhere around the nation and the world where the Lord sends me to minister. Pastors and their wives, along with hundreds of people in their congregations, are starting to experience these awesome face-to-face appearances from Jesus that are changing their lives and revolutionizing their walk with God so that they are experiencing Jesus in a relationship that they never knew was possible.

In the Church, we are clear that Jesus said, *"For where two or three are gathered together in My name, there am I in the midst of them"* (Matt. 18:20). It is so much easier for us to believe that He will be in the midst of us personally where two or three are gathered, than it is to believe He will be with us when we are alone. I know Christians today who are not conscious even of this very fact that, wherever two or three are gathered in His name, Jesus promised to personally be there among us! This is one of the first promises that I stood on in the earlier days of my Christian walk.

I was always looking for Him when I would go amongst other believers, for I took this Scripture literally and was always con-scious of this fact. As I mentioned earlier, sometimes during my personal prayer times I was not conscious mentally that Jesus was personally there with me when I was alone.

My eyes were opened when I found out that He not only promised to come in the midst of us when we gathered among two or three but also when we are alone. I had read in John 14:18 where He said (this was not only for the disciples but also for us today), *"I will not leave you comfortless."* With His next breath, Jesus made a bold promise to us: *"I will come to you."* This is what I have stood on for years, and He has continu-ally kept His promise to me. This promise is yours today as well. Notice, He didn't specify a limited number of times. This Scripture implies that He can come to us many times. He says, *"I will come to you."* That's a promise you can hold on to, and that's a promise He will perform in your life. He is going to come to you. Be awaiting your face-to-face appearance from Jesus.

THIS FACE-TO-FACE RELATIONSHIP IS AN ETERNAL COVENANT BETWEEN YOU AND THE LORD FOREVER.

When the Lord knows you face-to-face, the Bible says this means He has set your face before Him forever. This is an eternal covenant of intimacy with Him. The psalmist said, *"And as for me, Thou upholdest me in mine integrity, and settest me before Thy face for ever"* (Ps. 41:12). David then turned around and said, *"Behold, O God our shield, and look upon the face of Thine anointed"* (Ps. 84:9). David understood and knew that he had this face-to-face relationship. The Lord knew David face-to-face, and David often spoke of this!

For David speaketh concerning Him, I foresaw the Lord always before my face, for He is on my right hand, that I should not be moved (Acts 2:25).

WILL YOU BE CALLED FOOL?

Called a Fool by Jesus for Not Believing in His Face-to-Face Appearances

Afterward He appeared unto the eleven as they sat at meat, and upbraided them for their unbelief and hardness of heart, because they believed not them which had seen Him after He was risen (Mark 16:14).

Then He said unto them, O fools, and slow of heart to believe (Luke 24:25).

Jesus Wants You to Believe in His Appearances

In these passages, we see that Jesus was very displeased with the apostles for not believing those who had seen Him or those sent to testify that He had appeared after His resurrection. Jesus is the same yesterday, today, and forevermore. Even today, He is still displeased when His people are slow of heart to believe in His resurrected appearances. The Bible calls this type of unbelief a manifestation of a hardness of heart in men (see Mark 16:14). Those who do not believe in this type of manifestation of the Lord are called fools by Jesus and are highly rebuked, upbraided, or reproached by Him. The original Greek word for this is *oneidizo*, which invokes the image of someone being reviled or railed at by a stern rebuke.[4] The message is simple—don't find yourself in this position with Jesus because you don't believe in His appearances. Believe Him today, for this level of relationship is yours!

The Fellowship of the Mystery

THIS FACE-TO-FACE FELLOWSHIP WITH JESUS IS A MYSTERY THAT HE WANTS YOU TO SEE.

Unto me, who am less than the least of all saints, is this grace given, that I should preach among the Gentiles the unsearchable riches of Christ; and to make all men see what is the fellowship of the mystery, which from the beginning of the world hath been hid in God, who created all things by Jesus Christ (Ephesians 3:8-9).

The Lord Wants All Men to See

The Bible says here that this fellowship has been hidden in God from the beginning of the world. This speaks of the hidden fellowship that God had in the beginning with Adam. The Holy Spirit here, through Paul, is plainly telling us that this fellowship with God that had been hidden is now being revealed today in our age. Paul states that it is the Lord's will for us to preach the mystery of the fellowship with God which causes all men to understand and experience it through Jesus Christ.

The unsearchable riches of Christ are found in this mysterious fellowship we had before the Fall that has been hidden in God the Father. There were different men in the Bible who had the grace to go before the face of the Lord to prepare the way or arrange a special face-to-face appearance meeting between God and the people. This was Paul's calling and assignment from the Lord. God used another person to prepare us for the face of the Lord Jesus—John the Baptist. The Bible says John went before the face of the Lord to prepare a people to see the glory of the Lord when He came to earth in the face and person of Jesus Christ (see Matt. 11:7-11). The Bible records that the Lord sent John to prepare the way so that His glory would be revealed, causing all men to see it together (see Isa. 40:3-5).

The Hidden Fellowship
It Has Been Hid, but Now Is Being Revealed

Moses also had this anointing when Scripture says he brought the people to meet with the Lord and talk with Him face-to-face (see Exod. 19:17). He could not give away what he was not experiencing himself with the Lord. The Bible says that the Lord talked with him face-to-face in fellowship *as a man speaketh unto his friend,* and he had the ability to bring the people of Israel to meet with God in this same way (see Exod. 33:11; Num. 14:14). Jesus had a greater ability than Moses did to bring us into a face-to-face intimate experience with the Father. Moses did not see Jehovah God the Father face-to-face, but Scripture records that Jesus has.

Jesus Himself spoke of having seen the Father face-to-face, saying that this is why He could declare who the Father is (see John 1:18; 5:37; 6:46). Moses saw the form and likeness of God's shape and His back parts, but He did not see God's face (see Num. 12:8).

But Jesus has seen the Father face-to-face, and that's the glory that He prayed over us and wants to bring us into by arranging a meeting with God the Father (see John 17:5, 22-26). Right now, I'm not ready to talk to you about this level of relationship with the Father, but I will mention this later on in the book.

I want to keep you focused on the face-to-face relationship with Jesus first. This is the same thing the Lord has commanded me to do by writing this book and giving a record of my face-to-face fellowship and experiences with Jesus as He has appeared to me. So it is no new revelation that God would use a man to arrange this type of meeting. I have a similar grace and call from God upon my life to make all men see what the fellowship of this mystery is about through an intimate, personal face-to-face experience with the Lord.

The Fellowship Revealed

He Just Wants Things to Be As They Were in the Beginning

God values His first relationship and the first love He had with mankind in the beginning. He just wants it to be the way it used to be; that's all He wants. In the beginning, He was face-to-face with Adam. God used to come every morning, walking in the cool of the day, talking and fellowshiping with Adam face-to-face. He wants this relationship with mankind to be back the way it was more than you do!

The First Love

The fact that Jesus mentions "first love" means He values that first love and relationship He had with us in the beginning of our walk with Him (see Rev. 2:1-4). He values the first love He had with us the same way His Father does. When the Lord said, *"Let us make man in Our own image and after Our likeness,"* they were all there—Father, Son, and Holy Spirit (see Gen. 1:26). Jesus was there and helped in the creation of man, for the Bible says, *"In the beginning was the Word, and the Word was with God, and the Word was God....All things were made by Him: and without Him was not anything made that was made"* (John 1:1,3).

The Bible is not very descriptive about the Lord's relationship with Adam before the Fall. There are hints of intimacy when God comes from Heaven and walks in the cool of the day to fellowship with Adam, and when God's mouth breathed life into Adam's nostrils at conception (see Gen. 2:7). We can imagine how intimate humanity's relationship was with God before sin entered the picture by looking at the Lord's relationship with different people in the Bible after the Fall. Think carefully. If God had the level of relationship we read about in Scripture with Abraham, Moses, and Enoch after the Fall, when men were in a life and state of sinfulness, and it was sin that separated us in our relationship with God, then what was it like before the Fall? How much more (before sin entered) did Adam enjoy his relationship with God! This is what Jesus came to restore—this broken fellowship!

The Way It Was in the Beginning
Destroying the Ignorance That No Man Can See God and Live

Adam had the most intimate, consistent relationship with God before the Fall that we could ever imagine. We get a hint that Adam enjoyed something with God that we couldn't after the Fall when the Book of Genesis talks about God giving Adam CPR by breathing into his nostrils the breath of life (see Gen. 2:7). God had to be face-to-face with Adam to do this. When Adam came alive instantly, the first person he saw when his eyes opened was God standing in front of him. Adam opened his eyes and was brought to life when God stood before him and blew His breath into him. We hear these tragic words in Exodus 33:20 when Moses wanted to enjoy this same privilege with God by seeing Him in His glory face-to-face. God responds by saying, *"No man can see Me, and live"* (see Exod. 33:20). Many of us don't understand how tragic these words were because we don't have any revelation of the fellowship humanity enjoyed with God in the beginning. You see, it was because of sin that we were separated from God. After the Fall, when mankind was born with a sinful nature, we were separated from God and all the face-to-face privileges that Adam had enjoyed with Him in the beginning (see Ps. 51:11).

> *Behold, the Lord's hand is not shortened, that it cannot save; neither His ear heavy, that it cannot hear: But your iniquities have separated between you and your God, and your sins have hid His face from you, that He will not hear* (Isaiah 59:1-2).

Sin causes God to hide His face from us. After Adam sinned, he couldn't enjoy the blessing he once had in the Garden nor the privileges of the face-to-face relationship with God that he once had. The

Scripture records that we were born in sin and shaped in iniquity when we were conceived in the womb of our mother (see Ps. 51:5).

God told Moses he couldn't see Him and live because sin had formed in his body when he was born and would result in death when Moses saw God. The Bible also declares that *the wages of sin is death*" (see Rom. 6:23). God only spoke to Moses about dying because of sin, but from the beginning it was not so, because we were created to live forever in a type of body that had no sin in it. Sin separates us from God, and the result of this sinful nature is death when we see God's face. At the time of Moses, the wages of sin had not been paid for. Jesus, through His blood, paid the wages for sin and as a result has redeemed this relationship (see Rom. 6:23).

He's Out! HE RIPPED THE VEIL AND CAME OUT PASSIONATELY TO FELLOWSHIP WITH US AGAIN!

Jesus, when He had cried again with a loud voice, yielded up the ghost. And, behold, the veil of the temple was rent in twain from the top to the bottom (Matthew 27:50-51).

His Passion for the Relationship Caused Him to Tear the Veil

When Jesus died on the cross, the Bible says the veil that separated us from the presence of God in the Temple was ripped in two. Do you know what it means for the veil to be ripped? You have to remember that the pure, raw presence of

God Almighty was behind the veil in the Holy of Holies. Only certain men who were designated by God, the high priests, could go behind the veil where God was, and if their hearts weren't right with God, they too would die. This rip in the veil basically shows God saying, "I've been waiting to get out of here to fellowship with My people again!" So after the sacrifice for sins was paid through the blood of Jesus, God ripped the veil with excitement as He came out to be with man, whom He once enjoyed.

He's out now, and you can enjoy the relationship that mankind once had with Him. This is what the Scripture means when it says, *"God was in Christ, reconciling the world unto Himself"* (2 Cor. 5:19). The main purpose of Jesus' whole life was to deal (by His cross) with the problem of sin that separated us in our relationship with God, thus causing a reconciliation in the relationship that sin had breached between God and man. That's why the veil was ripped! The cross of Jesus was not just about Him dying for our sins, but it was the end result that He died for, which was to bring us back into fellowship with God. It was all about the relationship, and it's still all about the relationship between God and man, Him and us. It's all coming back around to what we were created for in the beginning, and that was to have fellowship with God in an intimate face-to-face way.

TRUE ETERNAL LIFE AND SALVATION
IS ABOUT KNOWING THE LORD INTIMATELY.

And this is life eternal, that they might know Thee the only true God, and Jesus Christ, whom Thou hast sent (John 17:3).

From the beginning, man was created for fellowship with God, and His purpose for sending Jesus was not just saving us *from* hell, but saving us *to* Himself. God was in Christ, reconciling the world to Himself. The whole purpose and result of God sending His Son Jesus was for the purpose of relationship with man. We are His prize and joy. In turn, our prize and reward is that He wants relationship with us more than we can ever realize. We were created for relationship with God. He sent His only begotten Son all the way from Heaven just to use Him to mend the broken fellowship and relationship between God and humanity. This is why Jesus mentioned in John 17:3 that real, eternal life is knowing God the Father and His Son Jesus in an intimate way. Having an intimate knowledge not just about God, but with God through experiencing Him!

Mythbusters About Appearances From Jesus
They Told You a Lie...

I thought it important to destroy the ungodly lies and myths concerning seeing Jesus face-to-face that exist in the Church today. There are lots of religious people who will try to discourage you from believing that these types of experiences with God are possible, or that you can have a relationship with Him of this magnitude. People who have had face-to-face encounters in dreams with the Lord Jesus Christ have come to me and shared the responses and attitudes they've experienced from some saints. After a young man shared about a visitation he had from the Lord, his church told him that God doesn't do that today! In fact, they told him that the visitation was from satan. How ignorant and how horrible this is on their part. May God forgive them.

What other religious people might say is, "I've been a Christian for years, and I've never been visited by the Lord!" "That is just foolishness!" Many go further and make statements like, "Anyone who can see a spirit is full of devils; stay away from those demonic doctrines!" Religion will fool you into thinking this book is not from God because there will be people who will tell you that "People can't see God," or "God is not that personal." That's all a lie! Religious people will tell you, "That's not God," or "God only did that in the biblical times; He doesn't do that now." All of these statements are lies.

Even now, you're probably thinking, *God doesn't do this anymore,* but that's not the truth! If you recall, the religious people who killed Jesus 2000 years ago did not believe that God had sent Him to make a visible face-to-face appearance in the flesh. As a matter of fact, the same religious people of our day will try to kill Jesus again in your mind and heart by discouraging you from receiving Him in this way through visitation appearances. Open your heart to really receive the level of intimacy and relationship that the Lord wants you to experience with Him in your life.

Take hold of these visitations from our risen Lord just as the men and women in the Bible did after His resurrection. I know there will be some people reading this book who will question this message and will ask their grandmas, Christian friends, pastors, or anyone who seems to be spiritually mature, *"Have you heard of this before?* Or, *"Can Jesus really do this?"* I have heard some say, *"No, that's foolishness; Jesus doesn't do that anymore."* Or they will say, *"I've been saved for 30 to 40 years and have never seen Jesus."*

Just because they have not seen Him does not make their statements true. These people might not be as close to the Lord as you think if they have allowed these thoughts to inhabit their minds, especially if they have not based their beliefs on studying and learning God's word in this area. I have more news for you: just because people call themselves "Christians," do "things" at church, or are churchgoers, doesn't mean they have this level of relationship with the Lord Jesus Christ. Matthew 7:21-22 illustrates this. This group of people did God's work but did not have a relationship with the Lord. It's just like when you have a job. You go to work, obey your boss's commands, and then go home, but it's different when you are friends with the boss. You still obey their orders, but you might go out to eat afterwards, or your boss might come to your house and spend time with you on a friendship level.

That's the difference: friendship, intimacy, and communion. So be careful of the opinions and deceptive religious wisdom of people when you begin to have face-to-face visitations from the Lord. Don't let them tell you that this is not real. Like so many thousands of others who have seen Jesus, my life is a living witness and testimony of this very fact, that He is alive and that He will appear to you face-to-face as He promised.

FAITH PLEASES JESUS.

71

Bringing Clarity to Jesus' Words: Blessed Is He That Believes and Hath Not Seen

The mature in the Lord may say, "I don't have to read this book." They will go on further to say, "This is OK for unbelievers and babes in Christ, but I don't have to see Him to believe." This is partially true; you don't have to see Him to believe. Those who believe without seeing Him are more blessed, as Jesus said to Thomas, but He was referring to those who are in unbelief and doubt about Him and demand proof to see Him just to believe (see John 20:29). This face-to-face supernatural appearance from the Lord is not limited to one certain group or circumstance like in case of unbelief.

Yes, Jesus appears to unbelievers to get them to believe in Him as He did with Thomas, as He's doing with Muslims, and as He initially did with Paul, myself, and many others. In this case, a face-to-face experience has nothing to do with whether you believe that Jesus has risen from the dead or not. It goes beyond this. You must realize that there is an ongoing relationship He wants to establish with you, person-to-person, face-to–face, and mouth-to-mouth. Seeing Jesus has to do with your level of intimacy with Him. Your Creator wants this relationship of intimacy with you. You must be willing to receive this gift that He wants to give you as a Christian by not limiting Him, or allowing religious strongholds through the false, ignorant opinions of supposed scholars of the Word of God to hinder you.

The type of men who deny that this level of relationship concerning Jesus appearing to people face-to-face are those who, the Bible says, are *ever learning but not ever coming to an experiential knowledge of the truth about what they teach*" (see 2 Tim. 3:7). The

Bible says they are ignorant and arrogant (see 2 Tim. 3:2-7). First, they are ignorant, and they innocently don't understand because they never had knowledge through an intimate experience of this face-to-face relationship. So they cannot give witness to the truth. They can be ever learning but not able to come to the knowledge of this truth by experience.

Second, the Word says that they are arrogant because they resist and oppose face-to-face encounters. Pride sets us at war with God, thereby rendering His judgment to resist and oppose us when we are proud. Humility allows the grace and favor of the King's countenance to be bestowed in your life so that you will see Him in this way with your own eyes when He comes and appear to you by the Spirit. The Lord is telling me that. Even pastors and leaders who don't understand this shall be visited. The Lord allows His mercy to rejoice against His judgment. Thanks be unto God for this unspeakable gift of allowing us to know His Son in this face-to-face way. Who wouldn't want a relationship with Jesus like this!

ENDNOTES

1. "Emphanizo": see http://www.studylight.org/lex/grk/view.cgi?number=1718; http://www.antioch.com.sg/cgi-bin/bible/vines/get_defn.pl?num=0138#A5.

2. Merriam-Webster's Collegiate Dictionary, 11th ed., s.v. "Keep."

3. "Paniym": see http://www.studylight.org/lex/heb/view.cgi?number=0644.

4. "Oneidizo": see http://www.studylight.org/lex/grk/view.cgi?number=3679.

How to Become a Personal Face-to-Face Friend With Jesus

He'll Be a Friend to You

How to Become a Personal Face-to-Face Friend With Jesus

Face-To-Face Friendship With Jesus

I really didn't know how I had become the Lord's friend so quickly after I had the visitations that I described in Chapter One. I thought to myself, "How did I become His friend?" You see, I never presumed that I was a personal friend of Jesus like I've heard so many Christians loosely quote when they say, "I am a friend of God." In this chapter, I would like to show you how I became a personal, face-to-face friend with Jesus, how it was actually attained. This relationship is not limited to a select few. You can be the Lord's friend in this way, a friendship that can be manifested evidently to yourself and to others openly. I will also explain how this relationship was established so quickly between us so that you can well be on your way to experience Him like this also. I am not going to tell you about these visitations in sequential order. Instead, I'm writing from the scriptural perspective I have now, twenty years later. I didn't have this perspective when I was young because I didn't understand what was happening to me. The Lord Himself has rebuked men on my behalf. He would appear to them and tell them that we were friends. These appearances didn't stop with the Caribbean pastor in 1992. Our friendship was also validated throughout my walk with the Lord through the ministry I did during my twenties. Before we move on, here are two more brief experiences of the Lord that validated our friendship.

Appearances That Validated Friendship

HE'LL BE A REAL FRIEND TO YOU.

Jesus Stood Up for Me, and Protected Me From Those Who Mistreated Me

He suffered no man to do them wrong: yea, He reproved kings for their sakes. Saying, Touch not Mine anointed, and do My prophets no harm (Psalm 105:14-15).

Have you ever met a real friend, someone who was true and loyal to you? That's what true friendship is about—being loyal and faithful to the one you're in friendship and covenant with. There is such a lack of true and ethical friendship in our society today. I have learned from my personal experience with Jesus that He is a true friend. I experienced the Lord's friendship on a firsthand basis again in 1997. There was a pastor at a church in St. Louis, MO, who started out as my friend until money got involved. This pastor turned on me and started accusing me of many things to his board secretly. When the Lord allowed me to find out, I couldn't initially believe he had said such things about me. Instead of responding poorly, in the flesh, I meditated on the words of Christ where He tells us to do good to those who do evil to us (see Matt. 5:44). I then confronted him on these things. I treated him with kindness, although he tried his best to hurt and slander my character. I then purposely gave this pastor a set of my most expensive furniture to be a blessing to him.

Before these types of judgments had begun in my life, I had learned and was obedient to Jesus' teaching about loving our enemies. I practiced doing good to those who were evil to me. I had learned to suffer while being wronged without using my prophetic gift or authority to bring the judgment of God on them. I even remember a time in college when one of my roommates hit me in my jaw. Boy, that really hurt! But instead of responding in anger or the flesh, as I would have done in my former worldly street ways, I turned my other cheek to him, as the Lord said for us to do in His Word. You see, I had meditated on Matthew chapters 5, 6, and 7 about the beatitudes and the way Jesus tells us to live with one another. I was obedient to this. So before these judgments started happening, I was just living normally as Jesus taught us to do. I was responding like I had always done since I was first saved. In the beginning, Jesus didn't ever stand up for me. But when he started supernaturally standing up for me, I learned later that I was in the beginning stage of my walk with Him. He wanted to see if I would obey His Word, and when I did He started disciplining and judging men on my behalf. It was totally unexpected on my part! No man was to do me wrong without consequences.

A lot of Christians are vengeful and want the Lord to vindicate them like this, but they have not passed the test of walking in genuine love toward their brothers, sisters, or enemies when they are wronged by them. They want God to judge other people who have wronged them or caused them pain in some way out of a spirit of anger, bitterness, and resentment because of what that person may have done to them. This is not Christ's way, nature, or character. After I passed those tests, He then promoted me as His friend to start walking in this realm of authority.

Jesus Appears to Me as the Head of the Church

The Chief Shepherd Appeared

And when the chief Shepherd shall appear (1 Peter 5:4).

One night during this same season, I was asleep when suddenly, without warning, I was whisked away with tremendous speed. I immediately appeared with Jesus, standing in mid-air over the roof of this pastor's church. Jesus had on the most beautiful white robe with the most firm look on His face, but He wasn't angry. He looked at me with great tenderness and held out His hand, extending it out in front of me. I stood on the right side of Jesus. I saw my feet and His feet though they didn't touch the ground or surface of the roof. He started pointing at the fingers on the hand he extended in front of me saying, "*You will be able to count the number of people who are left at this church because of what he has done to you and how he has mistreated you.*" I could see very clearly through the roof of the church below us. Then Jesus said specifically, showing me more plainly, that there would only be two rows of people left at that church. After this, I awoke! I knew that I had just been with Jesus supernaturally again. As quickly as He had come, He was gone. He was only with me face-to-face for a few minutes, and then suddenly I was returned back into my body.

The Chief Shepherd Defends Me as a Friend

The only word I could think of was *amazing!* He did that just for me! All I could remember were the words He said on my behalf to defend me in this visitation. This meant so much to me, not because Jesus was judging someone else (I hurt for this pastor), but because He did it for my sake. In this appearance, I saw Him act as the Chief Shepherd and Head of the Church, but we stood side-by-side as friends. I knew He was my Shepherd too, but in this visitation He acted on my behalf as a friend. This validated the friendship He spoke of five years earlier in 1992. I also realized then that there was something really special between the Lord and me. What I want you to understand is that this pastor's church was packed with people; it was full and running over. His ministry was beginning to boom, until he did this against me. I told him what Jesus said to me in the dream, and he didn't believe me. He said, *"I don't receive that,"* as if to give me the old cliché that the church uses when they don't want to receive a prophecy that they are against. But please remember that this visitation wasn't just a prophecy; it was Jesus in person and face-to-face, who the Bible calls the Faithful and True Witness of Heaven (see Rev. 3:14).

It was about three months later when everyone at that church suddenly left. Someone later told me that the whole church was almost empty. Without knowing about the visitation or what I had told the pastor, they said, *"There seemed to be only two rows of people left at the church on a Sunday Morning!"* This church stayed this way for at least two years. I felt so sorry for this pastor, but he was so stubborn that he wouldn't even hear about a visitation from the Lord Jesus.

Jesus Is Still the Chief Shepherd and Head of His Church

*For the husband is the head of the wife, **even as Christ is the head of the church: and He is the savior of the body*** (Ephesians 5:23).

What most pastors and leaders of many churches fail to remember is that Jesus is still the Head of the Church, while they are only under shepherds beneath His authority. Many pastors feel like they run God's house because they are the man set over that local work. They think that they have the last word, even about the church they pastor, but this is not true. The Bible declares that the Father has given Jesus to be the Head over all things in the Church, which is the Body of Christ.

And when the chief Shepherd shall appear, ye shall receive a crown of glory that fadeth not away (1 Peter 5:4).

*And hath put all things under His feet, **and gave Him to be the head over all things to the church, which is His body**, the fulness of Him that filleth all in all* (Ephesians 1:22-23).

And He is the head of the body, the church: who is the begin-ning, the firstborn from the dead; that in all things He might have the preeminence (Colossians 1:18).

In this visitation, Jesus was acting as the Head of the Church, and as what the Bible describes as the Chief Shepherd. It dawned on me that in this dream we were standing above the church, which symbolizes a position of superiority and pre-eminence. The Church is Father God's house which Jesus mentions in Mark 11:17. The Father has turned over His house into the hands of His Son Jesus in this day and age. In the Old Testament, the Father was head over the temple. This is seen in the Old Testament when He would send a word by the prophets to the leaders who were out of order. I began to see similarities be-tween the way the Father dealt with His Church in the Old Testament and how Jesus acted in this appearance. Jesus said that He does what He sees His father doing, and now I can truly attest that I have seen this firsthand in a face-to-face ap-pearance (see John 5:19-21). You may ask, "How?" In the Old Testament, one of the Father's judgments against the shepherds was that they would scatter and drive the sheep away. The sheep would then leave the erring shepherds behind, and the Lord would lead them to another fold or another shepherd.

And I will gather the remnant of My flock out of all countries whither I have driven them, and will bring them again to their folds; and they shall be fruitful and increase. And I will set up shepherds over them which shall feed them: and they shall fear no more, nor be dismayed, neither shall they be lacking, saith the Lord (Jeremiah 23:3-4).

This is what Jesus was doing in this visitation. He was showing me how He was going to scatter the sheep because of this pastor's offense. In this context, the Lord called the sheep, "My flock," which designates personal ownership. What we, as pastors, must realize is that the sheep are God's flock, not ours. The people are His, and He can turn them where He wants them to go!

A TRUE FRIEND WILL LET NO ONE SPEAK AGAINST YOU.

The point I'm trying to make here is how loyal Jesus is to you when in a face-to-face friendship covenant with Him. When He's your friend, He's your friend! He will not allow others (even those who claim to be His anointed servants or His children) talk behind your back and harm you with words. He will be loyal in His friendship with you. This level of relationship with Jesus is available to you, and He wants this so desperately with you. Well, what about you? Are you ready to experience this, or something like it?

Again, this experience changed my life. This awesome but sad demonstration of His judgment toward this pastor helped me become aware of how much Jesus loved me. The Bible speaks about the men who the Lord was in friendship covenant with, and how He judged and rebuked kings or anyone else who mistreated them. This happened with Abraham concerning King Abimelech (see Gen. 20:3). Also with Jacob. God defended Jacob to Laban by rebuking him in a dream (see Gen. 31:24). The Lord also stood up for Moses by rebuking Miriam and Aaron, his own blood sister and brother, for disrespecting him (see Num. 12:1-8). This also happened when God the Father and the Holy Spirit spoke on behalf of Jesus when dealing with Pilate and his wife. The Lord warned and rebuked Pilate and his wife through a dream not to have anything to do with crucifying Jesus (see Matt. 27:19). The Lord also spoke up for Paul supernaturally to Ananias, who was a Christian disciple who doubted Paul's character, integrity, and conversion (see Acts 9:13-16). And He will do the same for you!

Jesus Stands Up for Me Again

As my relationship steadily grew with the Lord, He didn't allow any man or circumstance to wrong me. When I say He has been a friend to me, I can truly say this because of the dramatic experiences that I've had. I never asked Him to do this on my behalf. It just started happening. Before this time, I was just focused and caught up in pleasing Him by loving and obeying Him. I have had to suffer persecution, but Jesus was still faithful.

I had another experience in 2001 when I was leading a service. The presence of God was thick and rich during worship when I saw Jesus appear over to the left side of the room. He wasn't walking; He was just standing there. When I saw Him (even though the people didn't), I turned fully toward Him to give Him my attention when He starting talking to me. He said, *"Do you see this young man on the front row?"* I replied, "Yes, Lord." There were a number of people in this service, but there was a young man on the front row who had a back brace on that covered his entire back reaching almost down to his hips. This brace was very noticeable and big.

He had come to get healed. I didn't totally know why he was wearing a back brace, but it looked very serious. Jesus continued talking to me about this young man saying, *"He is in this back brace because I'm judging him for speaking evil of you at different churches."* He said further, *"Tell him that if he will repent to Me and you for doing this I will heal him, and he will be completely healed in the morning."* I didn't even know that this young man had been going around saying evil things about me. He shared later how he had been out of work for two months because of his back.

So I went up to him and called him out in front before the people, and I started telling him everything I had just heard Jesus say to me. I had already told the people that Jesus had appeared in this service and was standing on the left side of the room. As we both stood in front of the congregation, I told the young man what the Lord told me about him. The Lord had instructed me to do this openly in front of the people because this man had spoken evil openly to many people.

Before this time, I had never openly done anything like this to anyone in service. I then stopped and asked him, "Is this true?" He responded, *"Yes,"* in front of the people. This young man then went on to tell me that he had been going around to people in different churches in St. Louis speaking evil of me, and putting down the ministry that the Lord had given me, because he didn't understand some things about my life and ministry. He then humbled himself and repented openly asking the Lord to forgive him, and then also asked if I would forgive him for the things he had said against me. He also said that there was no way that I could have known what he was doing unless the Lord had revealed it to me.

Then as I prayed for him, the pain left his back, and the back brace came off that very moment. He was totally healed! We still have pictures of this young man and his back brace. The next morning he went back to work. He was a log cutter who picked up heavy trees. You can't do that type of work with a bad back. Later, he shared how his back became like this, and he said, "All of a sudden one day my back just gave out on me, without warning or injury, and I started to have excruciating pain." He then continued, "I went to the doctor, and they could not find anything wrong with me, so they sent me home with this back brace. I have not been able to work for two months. The doctors couldn't do anything for me, so they put me in this brace and sent me home." He was so happy that he had repented and obeyed God. He said later that it was like a heavy burden had been lifted off him. This was another display of the Lord's love and friendship shown openly toward me. The people who saw this in that service were astonished and glorified the Lord! I was also very happy that the Lord had healed this precious young man and that he was humble enough to repent, unlike some other people who were stubborn and who had to experience the consequences of the Lord's full judgment!

How All This Began
Catalysts in My Love for Him

Some people have asked me, "How did you get this relationship with Jesus on this face-to-face level, and on a continual basis after your initial visitation from the Lord at your conversion? How do I have the same?" To be honest, I stumbled into this ongoing face-to-face relationship with Jesus through my decision to love Him which was inspired by His love toward me first. After the initial face-to-face appearance, I didn't have any knowledge or grid for what was happening to me, or how it was happening to me, as I do today. All I knew was that it just started happening. Years later, the Lord started showing me why it took place. These ongoing appearances kept taking place after the initial visitation. This first appearance from Him was totally by His grace and love for me, and not because of any love I had for Him. Before I knew it, this love captured me, causing me to respond to Him with love in return.

Because He First Loved Me

The Lord showed me the key reasons that caused these continual, awesome, face-to-face experiences to occur. These components caused the first appearance with Jesus to turn into an ongoing face-to-face relationship. A few days after my initial conversion, I was totally caught up and enraptured in Jesus' love for me. As I told you in Chapter One, the glory of God was so awesome in my room that I would rush home just to return to a place of prayer, communion, and fellowship with Him. There was also a brief experience that I haven't mentioned that led to all of this. It was my experience with the Lord's love. He allowed me to know, feel, and experience His personal love. This is the love that the Bible speaks of when it says, *"and to know the love of Christ, which passes knowledge."* Notice that it didn't say to know the "love of God" but rather to know the love of Christ (see Eph. 3:19).

The Lord wants us to know the love of God, but the point that I'm trying to make is that there's a distinct difference between the love of God and the love of Christ (see Rom. 5:5). I will explain this later. In the first days and months after my conversion, I would experience the Lord's love through a certain worship song that I listened to over and over again. This song would minister the Lord's love to me in a way that was ecstasy! The Lord used these songs of worship and adoration to inspire and stir my love and passion for Him. In the beginning of my walk with the Lord, worship songs of His sacrifice and love would stimulate my passion for Him every day. Every day I would sit by the radio and listen to a particular worship song called, "Lord, We Thank You," by the Mississippi Mass Choir.

As I listened to this song, I would meditate on the Lord—on who He was and what He had done for me in His sacrifice and death on the cross. Tears would course down my cheeks every time I played this song over and over again as I thought about the sacrifice He made for me. I was feeling His presence. I felt so appreciative and grateful to Him doing this for me. This softened my heart and brought it to the point of tenderness toward Jesus. It made me want to love Him in return, and to do whatever He would ask of me. After experiencing these intense moments of ecstasy, I thought to myself, "He couldn't ask me fast enough to do anything!"

He Promised to Circumcise Your Heart to Love Him

And the Lord thy God will circumcise thine heart...to love the Lord thy God with all thine heart (Deuteronomy 30:6).

By this process of the Lord loving me, He was circumcising (cutting deeper into) my heart for me to love Him in return. He was fulfilling His promise to circumcise my heart, and I didn't even know it. The Bible also goes so far to say that the Lord gets excited and rejoices over us with singing. The Bible says, *"The Lord will again rejoice over thee"* (Deut. 30:9). It also states that, *"He will rejoice over thee with joy; He will rest in His love, He will joy over thee with singing"* (Zeph. 3:17).

When the Lord sings and rejoices over us in His love, it really happens! When you hear a spiritual song playing in your heart over and over that you have no control of, it's really Him singing to you. This usually happens in the morning, or after coming out of God's presence in prayer. Isn't it awesome for the Lord to sing over us in His love!

As I mentioned earlier, this is more of what my prayer time consisted of—communion and fellowship with Jesus by putting on a slow spiritual worship song that focused all of my attention and thoughts on Him. When the beauty of the Lord was revealed through His presence in the room, a feeling of intense ecstasy and glory would engulf me. I was enraptured again in His presence and love. I would experience the touch and intense presence of God every day after the first week Jesus appeared to me by thinking or meditating on Him as this song ministered His love to me. This is also what you need as a Christian. Before you read any farther, it would be best that you get into God's presence by first letting Him touch you through song. Get a worship CD or a certain song that causes your heart, mind, and soul to experience His presence and love. This will prepare you and mold your heart to be able to fully receive the presence of God while reading this book. It will also prepare you for a face-to-face visitation from Jesus.

As I've seen in the Body of Christ, most of us are so into warfare prayer, intercessory prayer, and so forth, that we've forgotten that all of these different types of prayers first flow out of the prayer of communion, intimacy, and fellowship with the Lord. It's not the other way around. Our relationship and intimacy with the Lord is what gives us the anointed ability to be effective in these various assignments in prayer.

Abiding in His Love
How to Have Intimate Time With the Lord

Get somewhere alone and quiet. Then find a worship song (not just any worship song) that affects you in causing you to think upon the Lord—who He is and what He's personally done for you. Let His love minister to you. By doing this, you are doing what Jesus said in John 15:10, *"abiding in His love."* When you find this song, keep it close, and use it every day. You must be focused while it is playing to keep your mind on the Lord, on what the song is saying, and on the thoughts that the Holy Spirit will bring to your mind about Jesus that glorify Him. You must find the worship songs that will affect you in an intense way and that bring the level of brokenness in your heart causing tears of love and appreciation to erupt from your very being. You may say, "Why use songs that move me to tears?" The reason is that there is an intimacy and expression of love from our soul and spirit toward God that can't be put into words.

So instead, God has allowed us the privilege to express our love toward Him through tears and weeping. These tears act as a form of adoration prayer toward God. It's a privilege to cry, weep, and feel this intense ecstasy from God's presence during worship. There are some who will say, "Well, I don't cry, and I haven't shed a tear in years." Others say, "I'm just not a weeper or the type who cries." This mind-set is deceiving. God has made us all human, and He has put into us the ability to cry, shed tears, and weep for a purpose.

The Bible states several purposes for our tears. First, our tears serve as prayers toward the Lord, and when we cry, He preserves our tears by putting them into His personal bottle (see Ps. 56:8). The Bible also records that the Lord takes notice and sees our tears (see Isa. 38:5). The Lord also tells us that weeping helps us to turn toward God (see Joel 2:12). The Scripture even records that the Lord Jesus sought His Father with tears to find a way around the cross during His prayer in the Garden of Gethsemane (see Heb. 5:7). Weeping releases your love and emotions to the Lord in a way that your spirit or body can't. Your tears are prayers. Tears are from the soulish side of our makeup, and it is the expression of our soul loving the Lord. This is a command from God.

Your Tears Are a Part of Your Expression of Intimacy to Him.

The Scripture implies that we are to love the Lord our God with all of our soul, not just our heart, mind, and strength (see Matt. 22:37). Tears are what God has given us as human beings to express the way we feel and to release our affectionate emotions to Him. If you are human, you can cry, unless there is a physical ailment or sickness that won't allow you to. When the presence of the Lord comes into my room or in a service, I can't hold back the tears just from knowing the beauty of who He is and what He's done for me. His presence brings such a feeling of intense ecstasy that it causes me to weep profusely and sob. It's a wonderful feeling and a glorious experience with Him. I know that many of you reading this book now know exactly what I'm talking about.

HE'S SO PASSIONATE ABOUT YOU!

Someone may ask, *"Out of all the years of walking with the Lord, what are the things that are most dear to Him?"* My answer to that question, as I have seen from standing in front of Jesus face-to-face hundreds of times, would be *"you."* You are His primary concern. He prizes you and loves you with a love that you could never fathom. What I've seen from Jesus' conduct and character over these many years is how much He loves humanity. This is second to pleasing His God and loving Our Father. He loves the Father so much! May I love God like this? Help us, Jesus! I'm in tears now writing this. You matter to Him. You say, "I know that Jesus loves me." No, you don't! You don't know how much, how deeply, and how thoroughly He loves you. It's beyond knowledge and understanding!

I Saw How Much He Really Loves Us in His Eyes

He loves you so much that it's incomprehensible—beyond knowledge. After seeing Him, if a little child came to you to say,

"Jesus loves you," you wouldn't be able to say, "Yeah, I know," in pride and arrogance, because after seeing Him face-to-face, you will know that you don't have any idea how He loves you. Agape love from God doesn't necessarily always love us the way we want to be loved, or how we think we should be loved, but rather the way we need to be loved. If anyone had come to tell me that He loved me after I had seen Him face-to-face, my response would have been totally different. I realized I didn't know how deeply He loved me. After hearing this in His voice, I've seen how much every detail of your life matters to Him. The Scripture that says that *the very hairs of your head are numbered* has more meaning to me since I've seen the Living Word—Jesus—in action (see Matt. 10:30). He does love this way. This is why He gave His life and shed His blood on the cross 2000 years ago.

He's just that passionate about you now! We can understand from His sacrifice how He loved us back then, when He died for us, but I want you to understand how passionate He is about you now. Believe this and understand this. This is why He commanded us to continue in His love (see John 15:9). I have seen how passionate He is about you. He really cares about your heartaches and your problems, from the details of your life to the simplest of things. Pride, hate, and hardness of heart keep us from understanding this or even fathoming it. These things prevent us from experiencing or realizing His love in this way! You can depend on Him. You can lean on Him because He'll understand—for you matter to Him!

His Cross—His Passion
Jesus Showed Me His Passion and Love in Dying for Us on the Cross

The Lord took me back in time to the point and place of the crucifixion in a visitation that occurred in 1993. The only way I can explain this was that it was like getting into some type of time machine. I was taken back to the time and place of the crucifixion, but no one was able to see me there. Jesus took me back there and allowed me to watch. I saw how He was sent all the way from Heaven just to die for my sins and the sins of future generations. As I stood there and watched, Jesus hung there on the cross bleeding and suffering.

I saw His love. I saw His passion. Then the Lord started talking to me, saying, "I brought you here to see how much I love you, and not only you but the whole world. I love them, and I gave My life and love for them by shedding My blood on this cross that they shouldn't die." Looking at this and thinking of this caused me to weep and cry uncontrollably. I could not hold back the tears when I saw Him express His love to me. He showed me in real life by transporting me to the past to literally relive the actual moments of when He was hanging on that cross. Blood was all over Him. As I looked at Him, it was a terrible sight, but at the same time, a wonderful feeling of love and emotion arose as Jesus expressed His reason for the suffering and pain He endured. I saw His sacrifice and passion for us.

HIS LOVE, COMPARABLE TO NONE

I could not hold back the tears as I watched His torture and suffering—it was a horrible feeling inside of me, and I could not hold back the tears. Even at the beginning of my salvation, I always cried uncontrollably when I just thought about His sacrifice for me on the cross. It was wonderful! I wept in thanks, appreciation, gratitude, and love for what He did for me. The love that I saw at the beginning helped prevent me from going back to the world of sin at the time. It was this love that made me glad. I love and appreciate Him so much for what He's done for me that I want to love Him by living for Him and pleasing Him. As a result, I was ready to give up everything for Him because I saw how greatly He loved me. It was personal. I knew He died for the sins of the whole world, but He loved me. His love overwhelmed me, and I couldn't stop weeping.

I was out of control emotionally. I could not pull myself together; I'm crying now just writing about what took place. It was ecstasy! Actually seeing Jesus hanging on the cross caused me to feel the way that this song describes:

Down from His glory,
Ever living story,
My God and Savior came,
And Jesus was His name.
Born in a manger,
To His own a stranger,
A Man of sorrow, tears, and agony,
Oh, how I love Him! How I adore Him
My breath, my sunshine, my all and all!
The Great Creator became my Savior,
And all God's fullness dwelleth in Him![1]
Yes—He's my all and all!

He Allows Me to Feel and Experience His Love

Describing His Love

I was experiencing His love. It felt the same way it did when I would pray, and when the presence of the Lord would come into my room. It felt like a very warm bucket of liquid light that was poured on my head and whole being—it is almost totally indescribable. It was an overwhelming gentleness in which I was overcome with love, compassion, and mercy. God was pouring these things out on me even after I had made some of the most horrible mistakes in my walk with Him.

It was glorious. He loved me beyond my faults, shortcomings, and sins. I was overcome with His love. I was enraptured in serenity and relief that He still loved me after my mistakes. On earth, those who knew of my failures and faults, even those closest to me, deserted me. He was still there. He never left, and I saw that He was still in love with me. Nothing had changed in His eyes, or face, for me. I was undone; I was fascinated with this love He demonstrated. I said, "But Lord, look at what I've done and the many mistakes I've displeased you with." Then He lovingly and tenderly responded, *"I've forgiven you, David. It's fine; it's OK!"* His love was so full of peace: so calm, peaceful, mild, and tender. It was very loving and beyond description. When He loves me, it makes me want to love Him in return. We didn't first love Him; He first loved us! When I see His love toward me, it makes my whole being respond, saying, *"What do You want me to do, Lord? What can*

I do that would really please You??" One day after asking Him this in a face-to-face appearance, He replied to me with His gentle voice, *"Just love Me, David. That's all...just love Me."*

His Love Makes It Easy

I have shared with you about His intense love visiting me for three years. Then the challenge came to me to prove my friendship to Him. His love had, by this point, so engulfed me that my heart was ready to do anything that He asked of me. This love from Him numbed and blinded me to even knowing that I was making a sacrifice for Him. This made the challenge not feel like a challenge; instead, it felt like a privilege and an honor. I later learned that I had already obeyed His requirements for friendship before I even knew what was happening.

So when He called me His friend I *"wist not"* that I had even made a sacrifice to be His friend. In other words, it served as an anesthetic that deadened any ounce of pain that could have been felt from my sacrifice. His love took me past the knowledge that I had even made a sacrifice to be His friend. Like the Bible says, "I wist not" (see Exod. 34:29). This phrase, *"wist not"* means, not to realize, perceive, or have knowledge that a circumstance has taken place. That's what the love of Christ does; it takes you past knowledge. This friendship was not based on works in my own strength. It was based on my motivation to obey Him because of the love He gave me. It was all born out of the love that was developed in my heart. That's why I say no man can love God until God has loved Him. You can't fulfill a command to obey God unless you abide in His love. That's what Jesus meant when He said, *"Without Me ye can do nothing"* (see John 15:5). The Scripture also declares that it is God who works in us to will and do of His good pleasure. The Lord commanded us to love Him, and this is His desire and pleasure, but the Scripture here tells us that He works inside of us the desire for His will and gives us the ability to fulfill it (see Phil. 2:13). He loved me first, and as a result I loved Him, and it caused me to do whatever He asked of me without hesitation.

I think of it as a sacrifice or requirement to have this friendship with the Lord. Love made the knowledge of what I began to experience, and for what reasons, obsolete. It caused me not to take into account the suffering or sacrifice that was required because I never felt it. I didn't realize at the time, not until years later, that I had fulfilled the initial command from the Lord in order to possess this friendship. He had told me in a dream to walk by faith and to give up my career goal of being a chef, to leave my father's house and city, and to go back to Charleston with nothing. I gave up everything—my career and what I owned at the time! I was excited to do this. I loved the Lord with all of my heart as a result of His sacrifice for me on the cross. I thought, *"Is this all I have to sacrifice after what He's done for me?"* I said, "I will gladly do this," and I wasted no time. The very next week I was off and gone. I also thought (as most young ministers do) that the real ministry that the Lord had for me was about to begin, but in reality this was a long way off. Immediately following my obedience to surrender all, these dramatic validations of our friendship from the appearances of the Lord began taking place. I have written down the process that Jesus spoke about in Scripture that explains what Jesus requires of us to have this type of friendship with Him. I am telling you this so that you can duplicate this process. My story will act as a guide to the process.

How to Become His Friend

Discerning if You Are a True Friend of God

What Is Your Relationship With the Lord?

In the church today, we sing songs like, "I'm a friend of God," or make statements like, "God is my friend." Certainly I love praise and worship and especially that song by Israel Houghton, "I am a friend God." I've always loved the praise and worship that the Lord channels through Israel Houghton. Because of my personal experience with Jesus face-to-face, and because I have studied His Word, I've found out that the way we use this phrase is very loose according to the Lord's standards, and without true biblical substance. I've also found out from studying Jesus' personal words (printed in red in my Bible), along with other scriptural examples and highlights from the patriarch's lives, that the one we call a friend of God is not always the one who God calls His friend. Let's take a deeper look at this subject according to God's Word. Let's look at the laws and requirements concerning true friendship with Jesus according to His standards.

Jesus said, concerning true friendship between Him and us, that

Ye are My friends, if ye do whatsoever I command you.
Henceforth I call you not servants...but I have called you
friends (John 15:14-15).

It is true that Jesus calls us friends, but you must have discernment and wisdom to understand what He means in this context. You see, it's one thing for Jesus to call you His friend, but it's another thing for you to be a friend to Him. Let me explain. Jesus is a very kind and a friendly person. He will even look at His enemy as a friend. Remember when Judas came up to Him to kiss Him? What did He call Judas? A friend. Jesus said to Judas, *"Friend, wherefore art thou come?"* (Matt. 26:50).

You see Jesus makes Himself a friend toward everyone, but it's another thing when you are His friend! The point is, it's one thing for Him to be "your friend," but it's a totally different ball game for you to be "His friend." Jesus is always a real friend to you, but are you a real friend to Him? That's the question! Many pastors and leaders, who may be reading this book, have seen the Lord in dreams or in other ways. The Lord has already appeared to many of you, but like many pastors, you are quiet about this for different reasons. Some of you are afraid of sharing what you have seen. Then there are some who don't think they have really seen Jesus because they saw Him in a dream and don't think it was really Jesus, but only a vision of Him!

The Requirement and Condition

Jesus said, *"Ye are My friends, if ye do whatsoever I command you"* (John 15:14). The word *if* gives you and me a choice. Jesus' true test of our friendship is if we do whatever He commands us to do. Now, I'm not getting into legalism; I want you to understand a balance. Jesus being our friend is not predicated upon any good or bad we've done, but being His friend does have a requirement. Jesus loves us as we are right now—in our present state.

That's why He can be pleased with us in our process. There is another reward that He deems greater—when we meet the conditions of being a friend to Him. You see, Jesus longs to be loved by His creation. He's looking for love, and not only love, but faith which works out of love toward Him (see Gal. 5:6). This is why He was pleased with Abraham, who God named "the friend of God."

A True Friend of God

To help you understand this requirement that Jesus gave for us to be His friend, I must began showing you biblical examples of this great truth that the Lord revealed to me about true friendship with Him. If you notice, out of all the prophets in the Old Testament who lived and served God, including Adam, Moses, David, Jeremiah, and Malachi, the Lord never calls anyone His friend other than Abraham.

...*the seed of Abraham My friend* (Isaiah 41:8).

...*and he was called the Friend of God* (James 2:23).

The Lord showed me a great truth and spoke to me one day when I was pursuing a closer friendship with Him. He said to me, "David, it's not the people who called themselves My friend, but it's the person I called friend. It is the person I mentioned and leave on record that I consider to be a real friend to me." Then He said to me plainly, *"Abraham was My closest friend out of all the other prophets—even Moses!"* I said, "Lord, what do You mean?" Now I should tell you that up until this time I thought Moses was God's greatest friend, rather than Abraham, for two reasons. The first was because the Scriptures said, *"And the Lord talked with Moses face to face as a friend"* (see Exod. 33:11).

And secondly, I thought this because of how the Lord used Moses in comparison to Abraham, when it says, *"And there arose not a prophet since in Israel like unto Moses, whom the Lord knew face to face, in all the signs and the wonders..."* (Deut. 34:10-11).

I thought this because God talked with Moses face-to–face, like a friend, and He was used by God powerfully. This is not how God judges or tests true friendship with Him. As Jesus stated in John 15:14, true friendship with the Lord is proven only if you do *"whatsoever"* the Lord commands you. The words *do whatsoever* are the key. There are levels of relationships with the Lord. His friends are those who prove their devotion by doing whatsoever the Lord commands them, even if the ultimate test is to give up your life or the life of someone you love very much! This was the difference in Abraham's friendship with God. Even though Moses was known as being close to God, talking with Him daily in friendship, God never spoke of him being His friend at anytime as He did Abraham.

Friendship With God
Why Abraham's Friendship With God Was Greater Than Moses'

Abraham was recorded as God's friend because Abraham demonstrated the highest level of loyalty toward God in being a friend. When God tested and challenged Abraham to give up his beloved son, he obeyed God! The point is if you were going to use a person as an example, you would pick the person who demonstrated the best example. This is what God was doing when you find on record that, throughout the whole Bible, He called no one else other than Abraham, *"My Friend"* (see Isa. 41:8)! It's not that any of the other prophets were not God's friend to some degree, but only

Abraham demonstrated his love on a level of ultimate sacrifice and faith by trusting the Lord. And that means a lot in God's book!

The Bible says that He testified of who they were in His eyes (not the eyes of men), and He highlighted their strong points and heart toward Him during their whole life. For instance, we know both the Old and New Testaments record that Abraham was the "Friend of God." When Scripture speaks concerning Moses, God's testimony of him was different and highlighted a different aspect of his character. The Bible says many times that Moses was faithful in all God's house:

> *My servant Moses is not so, who is faithful in all Mine house* (Numbers 12:7).

> *Who was faithful to Him that appointed Him, as also Moses was faithful in all His house* (Hebrews 3:2).

Here's God's own testimony of David: "*I have found David the son of Jesse, a man after Mine own heart, which shall fulfill all My will*" (1 Sam. 13:14; Acts 13:22). This was awesome, and David had an intimate relationship with the Lord, but God's testimony of him at the end of his life was not that he was God's friend! Wow! Another would be Enoch: God's testimony and witness of him was that "*he pleased God*" (Heb. 11:5). He was translated as a result of walking with God and pleasing Him, and this is tremendous, but God does not call him *friend* as He called Abraham. Scripture never says that He was God's greatest "friend." So, do you see the point? We would assume that because of his translation, Enoch was the greatest example of friendship with God, but the testimony from God's mouth does not record this.

WHAT IS GOD'S TESTIMONY OF YOU?

Let me stop here and interject. My question to you is, what is God's testimony of you? What you must realize is that in spite of the failures of these men—David, Abraham, Moses—God still had a testimony and witness that was good about them at the end of their lives. God also has a good testimony concerning you that will be left on record to men. In some ways, God will manifest those testimonies of you to other men before you die. For instance, God said about David even before he was anointed *that he was a man after His own heart* (see 1 Sam. 13:14). God kept that testimony of him even after David's death. We see it mentioned in Acts 13:22 in the New Testament. The point is that God has a testimony of you that's good even if you have made mistakes like David, Abraham, or any of His other servants! Will you find out what it is? These examples that I'm giving you of my life in this book are just an example of what you can have and more. When the Lord initially started bearing witness of me to others, without my knowledge and outside my control, it all became clear. When He appeared to that Caribbean pastor and rebuked him, telling him I was His friend, it was then that I realized the closeness of our friendship. The Lord has a testimony of you, and the great thing is that you can hear God say it and know of it in this lifetime before you die!

The revelation of all this is: we should believe the testimony of someone who is recorded in God's Word, rather than our opinions or theological myths that have been created by men in their limited perspective. Our days are limited to 70 to 120 years. Will you not believe the Ancient of Days who has existed forever? Now let me explain why Abraham, in contrast to Moses, was a greater friend to God, and why his name was highlighted even after his death throughout the Bible. Now in the New Testament he is still known as being a *Friend of God!* When it came to the ultimate test of obedience for Moses and Abraham, Moses failed, but Abraham passed the test! Remember the law of friendship that Jesus gave in John 15:14 which says, *"You are My friends, if ye do whatsoever I command ye!"*

CAN HE ASK YOU TO DO *ANYTHING?*

The question is, can God command you to do anything, even that thing which you don't understand? Will you still love and trust Him when you cannot see where you are going? You see, Abraham had this pattern in his life from the beginning. Scripture records that Abraham went out (when he was commanded by God to leave his country and home) not knowing where he was going (see Heb. 11:8). Abraham had the heart to obey God this way. That was the foundation of him becoming God's ultimate friend! Remember this, Abraham is only an example and the starting point for us, but God has made it available for us to become an even closer friend than he was. God is not limited! Abraham's life and relationship was not the ultimate level, but it serves as a starting point and good foundation of where we can go in our pursuit of God. That's why when Jesus was on earth, He was really looking for friendship and relationship with us. He also wanted us to come after Him and pursue Him whenever He asked us to by being able to leave comfortable relationships with people He knew we loved the most. Most of us have ungodly relationships that hinder us from obeying the Lord when He tells us to do something. When we do, the rewards are high! Isn't that exciting! He wants this love and place in our lives from our hearts. That's why Jesus made statements like

> *He that loveth father or mother more than Me is not worthy of Me: and he that loveth son or daughter more than Me is not worthy of Me* (Matthew 10:37).

Being Found Worthy to Attain Him

When the ultimate test came to Moses in Exodus this was really the turning point that would decide not only if He would become God's friend but also if he would cross over into the Promised Land. As we know, when the ultimate command came from God to Moses to take the rod and speak to the rock, Moses failed to do so because of unbelief (see Num. 20:8-12). The children of Israel didn't cross over into the Promised Land for the very same reason—unbelief (see Heb. 3:19)! This friendship with God has a great deal to do with faith and believing in Him out of your love for Him. Remember what it said about Abraham, *"Abraham believed God, and it was imputed unto him for righteousness,"* and as a result, *"he was called the Friend of God"* (James 2:23).

It was Abraham's faith working by his love for the Lord that caused him to make the ultimate decision to give up his son, whom he loved. This would have meant giving up all the plans, purposes, and hopes that the Lord had given to Abraham through their covenant relationship regarding Abraham's son. For God said about Abraham that out of Isaac, *"so many as the stars of the sky in multitude, and as the sand which is by the sea shore innumerable"* (Heb. 11:12). Abraham did not flinch, or try to reason or argue with God about how or when the promise would be fulfilled. God was telling him to sacrifice and kill his son.

Abraham Passes the Ultimate Test of Friendship With God

The Bible records that Abraham believed God out of his love, trust, and security in the promise God had given him. By faith, Abraham believed God that the impossible could still be accomplished even after his sacrifice (see Heb. 11:17-19). He believed God could raise Isaac from the dead after he had obeyed God by sacrificing his son. Either way Abraham did not deviate from God's word of promise made to him about Isaac. Abraham believed God so wholeheartedly that after God commanded him to sacrifice Isaac, his mentality was, *"I know God's word and promise is so sure that after I kill Isaac, God has to raise him from the dead to fulfill His promise because He swore to me and He will not lie!"* What belief! What faith! You see, believing and walking in faith has a lot to do with you showing your love for God and obeying His commands. It takes faith to be obedient to God. We see Abraham did not fail this test, and afterward God told Abraham that He would bless him because Abraham had not withheld his only son, whom Abraham loved very much (see Gen. 22:16). Abraham passed this test in victory and was rewarded with a relationship with the Lord Himself. The Lord was his prize and exceedingly great reward and Abraham proved this by his actions. With Moses, though, this was not the case.

When the time came for God to test Moses in his faith, trust, and belief, he failed. He not only missed the reward of being called God's friend, but he also lost out on crossing the Jordan and entering into the Promised Land. Because of his unbelief, Moses had to be judged and taken home (to Heaven) early.

Moses Fails His Test of Deeper Friendship With God

God told Moses his mistake at the rock was because he failed to believe God and sanctify the Lord in the eyes of the people. For years I didn't understand this because I was taught, and believed, that Moses didn't enter the Promised land because of his anger and temper with the people. This was not true; God told him to speak to the rock, but instead Moses hit the rock with the rod. The Lord explained to me that Moses' unbelief was with the rod. You have to understand that every miracle, sign, and wonder that God did through Moses was with the rod—the plagues all happened when God told him, "stretch out your rod," and the Red Sea parted when Moses extended his rod. At this point, God was changing the command and strategy. God didn't want him to use the rod, but He wanted him to speak to the rock. Moses didn't believe that if he spoke to the rock that water would come forth. Remember that the Lord got angry with Moses for unbelief in the beginning when the Lord first called Moses (see Exod. 4:10-14). Moses was insecure because he could not speak well, and because he had a speech impediment. Moses had unbelief in the speaking realm, so he stayed with what was comfortable for him and what always worked—the rod. This ultimately caused him to miss out on the greatest blessing and promotion with God, not only in this world but in the one for all eternity!

An Unexpected Testimony From the Lord

At the turn of the twenty-first century, maybe between 2001 and 2002, I was encouraged by another face-to-face visitation from Jesus where He appeared to another person on my behalf. I couldn't understand why Jesus would go to others and say these wonderful things about me that I myself was still discovering I had with Him. I guess He wanted it this way, especially since His Word says, "*Let another man praise thee, and not thine own mouth; a stranger, and not thine own lips*" (Prov. 27:2). I also see that it was His way of humility, because it would have looked like I was the one who said that Jesus told me, "I am His friend." It gives more credibility for it to come from someone else's mouth to whom the Lord has appeared, especially your enemies. You know that you have something special with the Lord if your staunch enemies come back and apologize, saying that Jesus has appeared to them face-to-face in a dream, rebuking them and telling them that you are His friend.

JESUS WILL APPEAR TO YOUR CHILDREN TOO.

He Will Not Leave Your Children out of This

At this time, most of my staff was being visited by Jesus personally, in face-to-face encounters of which I will tell you about later. Their children were also being visited, having out-of-body experiences, taking trips to Heaven, and having face-to-face encounters with Jesus as well.

My heart is overjoyed that Jesus has appeared to both my two little children as well, who are nine and eleven years of age at the writing of this book. About two years ago, Jesus started appearing to both of them and taking them to Heaven. Jesus has appeared to both of them twice and spent personal time with them. This has made my heart so overjoyed because a face-to-face appearance with Jesus teaches a child what a parent cannot, that the Lord really exists. When a child, adolescent, or teenager starts to experience Jesus for themselves in this personal way, it makes all the difference in the world concerning the reality and impact of who Jesus really is. This is the effect of the face-to-face experience I had when I was eighteen, which immediately impacted and changed my life beyond all the years that my parents taught me about the Lord. Through the content of this book, Jesus will not only appear to you but to your children also!

It seems that when these visitations started happening to the parents, their children were also affected and impacted by the Lord also. I know of one little boy who must have gone to Heaven, because he couldn't have talked about Heaven the way he did if he hadn't been there. Heaven—I have been there, and have heard of other experiences of people going there as well. You must understand that I tested this boy to see if this experience that he talked about was really true, and it was. He was able to describe colors and details of things that only exist in Heaven!

For the sake of time, I won't tell you about his whole trip, but during the majority of the trip, Jesus walked him around Heaven and showed this boy, among other things, his personal mansion.

Jesus' Own Personal Mansion in Heaven

As Jesus took this young boy around Heaven, He then took him to His own mansion. When he told me this, I thought, *Jesus has a mansion?"* It hadn't dawned on me that Jesus ever had a mansion in Heaven of His own. I would think that He had a castle. I've been to Heaven and have heard testimonies from others who have also been taken there and who saw their own personal mansion and the homes of the prophets. But no one ever mentioned that Jesus showed them His own personal home. I only focused on all of Heaven being His, which eclipsed my mind from thinking He had His own personal mansion. I thought these mansions were just made by Him for us only. Then the Scripture came to me that said: *"And He is the head of the body, the church: who is the beginning, the firstborn from the dead; that in all things He might have the preeminence"* (Col. 1:18).

You see, all we focus on is that Jesus has told us that His Father's house has many mansions, and that He is going to prepare a place for us (see John 14:2-3). We focus so much on Jesus building us a mansion that we forget that He is the firstfruits, and has the pre-eminence to be first in all things. Jesus can build us mansions because the Father has built Him one. It's the same principle with Jesus rising from the dead—He had to rise first before anyone else could rise from the dead.

The Bible says that Jesus is the firstfruits of the resurrection (see 1 Cor. 15:20-23). Wow! Jesus has His own place! As Jesus took this boy around His home, He showed him the landscape of His yard. Jesus' backyard had a beautiful waterfall with crystal clear water flowing from it. It was so beautiful. This boy also told me that he saw how much Jesus loves lions. He saw real lions laying down and walking around in His yard. From the other details this boy described, Jesus' mansion was immaculate and astounding!

The Testimony
Jesus Compliments My Preaching

Jesus walked this little boy around Heaven, and at one point in their fellowship, Jesus turned to him and said, *"Tell David that I love what he preaches, because he preaches what I like to hear and not what the people want to hear."* I was so encouraged when this little boy sat me down and told me what Jesus said to tell me. Tears welled up into my eyes. I thought, "Wow, what encouragement!" Jesus likes to hear me preach! This had confirmed my fears and concerns that I had since the 1992 visitation where Jesus appeared to me and said, *"I need a man to stand on the authority of My Word."* What concerned me was the fact that He didn't say He had specifically chosen me to do it—He left it open to me to become the one who would stand on the authority of His Word. He never said to me, "David, I need you to stand on the authority of My Word." He said, "I need a man who will stand on the authority of My Word." This encouraging word brought me much relief for years to come.

The Honor That Comes Only From God

I am come in my Father's name, and ye receive me not: if another shall come in his own name, him ye will receive. How can *ye believe, which receive honour one of another, **and seek not the honour that cometh from God only?*** (John 5:43-44)

After reading these passages early in my walk with God, I have wanted the supernatural and divine honor that only God gives. It so encouraged me to hear this testimony! There are men who seek the approval of others more than they seek the approval and honor that comes from only God. But as you read later on, this testimony came years after great testing, trials, and judgments from the Lord. I've had many great men endorse other books that I have written, but the Lord told me not to have anyone endorse this book. He said that this was His honor. To have men endorse me in this book would be totally contradictory to the honor that comes from only God.

ENDNOTE

1. See http://www.hymnal.net/hymn.php?t=h&n=82.

CHAPTER 4

His Personality

Face-to-Face He Showed Me Who He Was in Person

CHAPTER 4

His Personality

What He's Like in Person

One thing that has distorted our view of Jesus is our inability to see and know Jesus in His divinity. When I speak of Jesus' divinity, I'm referring to His divine nature as God. Jesus' divinity refers to His external titles that describe what He does and who He is without revealing what He's really like as a person at heart. His divinity deals with who He is as the Son of God, King, Savior, Deliverer, Redeemer, and Healer. But none of these things tell us who Jesus is internally at heart or in person. They are all external classifications and titles of who He is and what He does. This is where the Church has been deceived, because they've only seen His glory in these external aspects of who He is. They have not been face-to-face with Him in person. In this chapter, I share the balance between who He is in

His divinity and what His personality is like in some of the face-to-face encounters I have had with Jesus.

HE'S MORE THAN A KING.

He's Emperor
Jesus Tells Me Who He and God the Father Are

In 1996 I had one of the most glorious experiences in all of the face-to-face encounters I've had and in all of the trips I have taken to Heaven. I didn't know it could get any better after all of the wonderful experiences I have had. I was dumbfounded. The closer I became to the Lord, the more He began to reveal to me about Himself and His Father, whom we call God. During this time, I was still growing and making a lot of mistakes. It is easy to think that you know a lot, especially when you're being mentored by spiritual fathers in so much revelation. Well, I thought I knew more than what I really understood because I was studying and learning the glorious revelation that God gave Benny Hinn, who is one of the greatest men of God living today. During this time I was learning more and more about the subject of the anointing. Pastor Benny had written a book called *The Anointing*, which is a great book that taught me volumes concerning how to walk in the anointing of the Holy Spirit in my personal life.[1] While studying this book between 1994 and 1996, I read about the three different stages of the anointing that we all go through after we receive Jesus as our personal Savior. Pastor Benny mentions in this book the leper's anointing that we receive when we get saved as a result of accepting Jesus. Then he talks about the priestly anointing that we receive after salvation as a result of spending time with Jesus. Then finally he talks about the kingly anointing that we all receive as saints by obeying Jesus! The kingly anointing was very intriguing to me. At this point, I had sought the Lord for six to seven years about His Kingdom, so this opened up more revelation and light concerning God's purpose for us through Jesus' blood. Pastor Benny also states in this book that the kingly anointing is the most powerful anointing of them all! I believed the same thing, like so many other western Christians who know little about the true nature of God's Kingdom. I didn't know what I'm about to share with you until I was taken to Heaven one night while I was sleeping. All I had been taught or had understood from growing up in America was that the realm of the king was the highest authority and anointing. This is all I had heard since I was a child. I had even heard taught from God's Word that Jesus was not only a king but He was the King of kings and Lord of lords. But during a trip to Heaven I was about to find out that He was even greater than this!

Jesus Causes Me to Appear Before Him Face-to-Face in Heaven

Suddenly and without warning or prior knowledge, I was again beamed or summoned into Heaven while asleep at night. I don't know how to explain this other than to say it felt like I was whisked or summoned, just like the speed of thought, and I was immediately in Heaven standing in front of Jesus face-to-face. In most of the experiences that I've read about, people have described the Lord sending a transport or angel to escort them to Heaven. From this, I understood that the way the Lord summoned me many times, when I stood directly in front of Him, was a special honor and privilege because of our close friendship. I saw how He did not send an angel or any other form of transportation for me to be escorted royally into His presence as He is rightfully a King. But He allowed me a personal audience with Him; I was summoned directly into His presence without the protocol. It took me years to fully understand the significance of these details that I had initially overlooked. During this encounter, I didn't realize the significance of Jesus standing in front of me face-to-face. At other times, He would be standing on my right or left. There He stood in front of me, over six feet tall with sandy-brownish hair, parted at the top, coming down the sides of His face to His shoulders.

GOD IS AN EMPEROR WITH AN IMPERIAL ANOINTING AND POWER.

I couldn't help but notice the beautiful white robe He had on that He wore most of the times that I had seen Him. Jesus looked me straight in my eyes and started talking to me, saying, *"David, I brought you here to give you a revelation about who My Father and I are."* Then He continued, *"You have taught wrong when you say that the kingly anointing is the highest and greatest anointing in the Kingdom. I brought you here to reveal a truth to you that the kingly anointing is not the highest anointing before you cross over into the dimension of My Glory."* He said further, *"This highest anointing is called the 'Imperial anointing.' It is the highest anointing in the Kingdom before you move out of the dimension of the anointing and cross over into the realm of the Glory."* Then He said, *"David, My Father and I are not just Kings; We are Emperors. This imperial anointing comes from the presence and authority of an Emperor just like the kingly anointing comes from the presence and office of a king."*

He said, *"This is the highest anointing in My Kingdom."* I was in awe as the King of kings and Lord of lords was lovingly and meticulously teaching me right in front of my very eyes. His correction and mild rebuke to me about what I had been teaching wasn't condemning, and although I knew it was, it didn't feel like correction at all. When correction is given in Heaven by the Lord, there is such a wholeness of God's presence that is unlike His presence on earth that you don't feel condemned or overwhelmed with guilt like you might if you received the same rebuke on earth. Then He began to teach me how to use this anointing for His Kingdom and how to operate in it by pointing out places in Scriptures where He had walked in this imperial anointing versus when He walked in His kingly anointing. He began to describe the difference between the imperial anointing and the kingly anointing by talking about how to pray for the sick. If a person comes in without eyeballs (just sockets in their head), the kingly anointing would say or command, "I command eyeballs to form," and eyeballs would form. The kingly anointing addresses what is out of order. Under the imperial anointing, which is a higher commanding ability (power), you wouldn't address the fact that the person doesn't have eyeballs in their head. Your command does not battle nor address what is out of order like the kingly anointing does. Instead, in the imperial anointing you would say what you want without addressing what is not. Instead of saying, "I command eyeballs to form," you would say under the imperial anointing, "Read this book!" and the miracle of eyeballs would have to form and be established to fulfill the command. Wow! This is what the Bible means when it says, *"Thou shalt also decree a thing, and it shall be established unto thee"* (Job 22:28). This implies that it is given to you, not that you have to battle and work to establish it!

Operating as Emperors Rather Than Kings

I learned years later that the kingly anointing would cause kings to go out to battle to put things in order, but the imperial anointing operates differently. An emperor rarely gets up off his throne to go to war or battle. He says or commands what He wants to happen! This is the anointing that Jesus was trying to teach His apostles and disciples to walk in when He said, *"Have faith in God,"* or better yet translated, *"Have the God kind of faith"* (see Mark 11:22). Jesus was teaching His disciples to operate in this anointing when He further said, *"If ye shall say unto this mountain, be thou removed, and be thou cast into the sea; it shall be done. And all things, whatsoever ye shall ask in prayer, believing, ye shall receive"* (Matt. 21:21-22). Jesus was teaching them and us to operate in the imperial anointing by telling us that we can have, *"whatsoever we say"* by command, instead of complaining and operating in unbelief and settling for what we have.

After I came back from Heaven, I looked up the word *imperial,* and to my surprise I made a shocking discovery. This word comes from the Hebrew word *shalat* which means, "to govern or to permit to have dominion and power."[2] This is what God said to Adam after first creating him in the beginning. When He said in the beginning, *"Let Us make man in Our image and after Our likeness and let them have dominion,"* He wasn't just making us kings but He was making us after His image as an Emperor (see Gen. 1:26). I also looked up the word *emperor,* and it comes from the Greek word *sebastos* which means, "august, reverent, or reverential awe."[3] The term was taken from the Roman emperor Augustus and is a title of honor. This word is also related to other similar Greek words meaning, *"to worship or venerate an object of worship."* This is why the Father seeks people to worship Him in spirit and in truth because He is an Emperor (see John 4:23). The word *imperial* also comes from a Latin word which means, "to command."[4] This is awesome because in many places the Bible speaks of God's nature in calling things into being. So in summary, an emperor is one you should have reverential awe for. God as our Emperor should be the object of our worship and reverential adoration. Imperial power implies the power and presence that an emperor carries, which denotes his ability to command with a specific level of great authority and power. An emperor's command is not like a king's command, but it is much greater and on a higher level! A king and an emperor both have the power in their mouth to command, but the level of authority and power by which their commands operate is far greater and farther reaching with the emperor.

Jesus was teaching us to have the Father's type of administration and faith. Jesus has imperial power and emperorship as the King of kings, but the Father is the Highest Emperor. Jesus Himself declared that He did those things that He sees His Father doing. The Father is Emperor, and this operation of His work is described in Scripture when it says, *"God, who…calleth those things which be not as though as they were"* (Rom. 4:17). This implies that God overlooks in faith the things that are not presently His desire, and He calls them what He wants them to be. He says what He desires and not what He presently has. Our God is an emperor, not just a king. This is also what it meant when the Bible says that God commanded (that was His imperial power) the light to shine out of darkness. Notice God did not battle, rebuke, or address the darkness; He only commanded the light! Wow!

Differences Between the Kingly and Imperial Anointings

The kingly anointing speaks to address and command the darkness which describes demons or things that are out of order. The imperial anointing is on such a higher level that it addresses what it desires the light to do in the midst of the confusion or darkness. It is so powerful that it is not bound or limited to focusing on what is wrong and out of order. It focuses more on what is desired. I know I've just mentioned this before, but I must say it again; this is what Jesus meant when He said, *"Have faith in God"* or "the God kind of faith." Then He went on to say, *"For if you shall say or command…."* (see Mark 11:22-23). The God kind of faith commands and calls those things that are not (the light, or things desired) as though they were. The imperial anointing causes you to act, command, and talk as though what you desire has already been established, even though it has not manifested at the present time! That's the point of the imperial anointing. It has the power to address the things that you desire. That's the imperial anointing!

The Imperial Anointing
How This Operated in His Healing Ministry

He then showed me how He walked in this anointing compared to times when He walked in the kingly anointing. For instance, He pointed out specific moments in His earthly ministry when He walked in His anointing and authority as a king, by rebuking, addressing, and casting out demons of sickness. He then said, *"Did you notice that I would rebuke and command evil spirits to leave some people and they would get well, and at other times, like the man with palsy, I walked in imperial authority and didn't address the demons, but rather commanded what I desired to happen to them? I didn't rebuke or address the spirit that had him bound with sickness. I strategically spoke to him declaring what I desired to see happen."* The Bible states that Jesus said to the sick man with palsy, *"Get up and go into your house,"* and the man was healed by this command! Wow! He did not rebuke an unclean spirit or demon in this situation as He had at other times.

YOU ARE ALSO NOT JUST A KING, BUT AN EMPEROR MADE IN THE IMAGE OF GOD.

Called by God and Jesus to This Anointing

This was an awesome revelation as Jesus stood face-to-face and explained this to me. He let me know He wanted me to teach this truth and type of anointing to His people by training them to operate in it. He also revealed to me that because God was an Emperor, and we as men are made in His image, that we too are not just kings, but emperors with this imperial anointing! He then said that He had commissioned and given this anointing to me to teach and release it upon earth to men. I thought, "Wow! The imperial anointing; what power!" You see, my friends, there is a place in God's presence where there is such power that you do not have to address or focus on devils or darkness. There is a place in God where demons will fall a thousand at your side and ten thousand on your right hand before they can even come near you. When I started walking in this level of anointing after coming back from Heaven, I saw greater and more dramatic miracles taking place in our crusades here in America and around the world. Immediately after this encounter, whole regions began to be transformed without me rebuking, addressing, or casting out demon spirits, and diseases in the bodies of people began to manifest healing without me addressing the sicknesses. Before this encounter, I would have had to rebuke demons with the kingly anointing. I still walk in this kingly anointing today when the Lord instructs me to address an evil spirit, but what I'm saying is that ever since this increase of anointing was given to me by Jesus, I don't have to address and battle evil spirits as much as I did previously. This imperial anointing is so powerful that it allows me to get more done for God's Kingdom by doing less work in battle against unclean spirits! For the sake of time, I cannot tell you everything that was taught or shown to me in Heaven about this subject, but that is why I've compiled books and CDs about these various revelations that were given to me by Jesus for this generation and for you as a believer. You can walk in this awesome anointing and change the destiny of whole regions and nations! You have been chosen to change the atmosphere with the Imperial Anointing.

He's a Person of Royalty

JESUS IS ALL GLORIOUS!

His Golden Robe—Clothed as the King of Kings

One night as I was asleep, Jesus came to me again. This time He was more beautifully dressed than I had ever seen Him. He didn't have the white robe on as He normally did when He would come to me. He was glorious. He looked like a very important person. He had on a beautiful satin-looking shining robe that draped over His shoulders and around His waist. As I looked closely, I could see that it was His King of kings attire and dress. This robe draped around Him down to His feet. He didn't have on shoes. He didn't do anything but stand in midair and look at me. I was so overwhelmed with the beauty and glory of these clothes of all-wrought gold.

He Was Dressed in Majesty

It was a golden robe that I had never seen Him wear. It was so beyond this earth. I had never seen clothes or a robe like this. He was regal in appearance. He had a royal stance. He didn't say a word to me, but He didn't have to. The splendid beauty of His glory said it all. Again, He was now more beautiful beyond description than I had ever heard or seen myself. I was again overcome. All I could think of was how in awe of Him I was, like that song says, "I stand in awe of You / Holy God to whom all praise is due / I stand in awe of You."[5]

Jesus' Style of Dress
Why He Wears the White Robe

Jesus showed me His King of kings garments. Most of the time when He comes to me, He is dressed in His beautiful fine linen white robe. I've noticed during my trips to Heaven that most of the people there, including Jesus, wear robes. I asked the Lord, "Why do you like wearing robes?" I asked because I had never seen Him dressed in jeans or a T-shirt like us. I had never seen Him in a suit and tie with pants like I wear here on earth. The Lord allows some people to dress in Heaven the way that they liked to dress on earth. He also does this with our homes and mansions in Heaven. He allows us to decorate our homes in Heaven with the style of furniture that we like. When you get to Heaven and see your own personal mansion that Jesus has built for you, it is laid out and built with your personal preferences, style, and taste. In Heaven all our desires are fulfilled.

Jesus Answers Me

He answered, when I asked Him why He dressed in robes, *"David, this is My personal preference, and My Father's."* From this, I found out that Jesus dresses in the white robe garment because this is His personal desire. He also has a bigger selection in His wardrobe of clothes, many of which I have not seen. He said to me, *"David, I have a massive selection of robes in different colors and different materials that you have never seen Me wear."* I then asked, "Lord, why then do I see you in this white robe most of the time?" He said, *"David, because I love this one the most."* I was shocked to know that Jesus has a massive wardrobe, but that He wears this white robe most of the time. I noticed that in most of my visitations and in those that I've heard others share about, Jesus always wears a white robe. Those of you to whom the Lord has appeared may have seen Him wearing this same white robe. His white robe has always been beautiful, but compared to this robe designated as his King of kings robe, it looked simple. Then I said to the Lord, "The white garment looks so simple compared to this one You wear." Then He replied to me, *"I am simple, easy, and lowly. I dress according to My heart, and out of My heart flow the issues of My life in the things that I wear."* Then He said, *"My heart is lowly."*

Jesus Is a Person of Style and Taste

I began to learn more and more about Jesus at this stage in my walk with Him. The Lord was constantly trying to break my wrong mind-set and myth about who He was and His personality. Like most Christians, I had a one-sided view of who I thought the Lord was and how He acted. I was taught in church the religious, starched view of who Christ is. So the Lord took me to Heaven in this face-to-face visitation just to show me a different side of who and what He is like.

You see, my friends, He is a very real person, just like we are, who has feelings, emotions, and preferences. We think that Jesus is this person who sits on the right hand of God in a starched position, never moving or not having any personality at all. But I have seen another side of Him, and He took me to Heaven in this face-to-face appearance just to show me. My trip this time to Heaven was not very long but simple and short. I was asleep again in 1998, when immediately I was taken out of my body to Heaven, and I was standing right in front of Jesus face-to-face.

HE CARES ABOUT THE DETAILS.

Summoned Into Heaven for Five Minutes
He Liked My Shoes

I was not standing beside Him like other times, but He was standing in front of me face-to-face. This happened so quickly, as if I had been zipped away in the twinkling of an eye, and was placed directly in front of the King, Jesus Christ. He started speaking to me, saying, "*I brought you here to Heaven just to tell you I like the shoes you wear.*" Then He went on to say to me, "*You're going to hit your foot up against something that will damage those shoes that I like, so I want you to go and buy another pair of them.*"

After Jesus spoke these words to me, I was then immediately placed back in my body here on earth and awoke. Now please understand that I was still very religious, and did not know Jesus the way I thought I did—just like most Christians. I struggled with the idea of this in my mind, thinking, "*Jesus couldn't like shoes; He's God!*" Then I started thinking more religiously: "*No, there has to be something wrong with this visitation.*" To help you understand the background of this story, I should tell you that I had bought some very nice shoes that I would wear while ministering to God's people during miracle crusades. I really liked these shoes, but had no idea that Jesus liked them too! I am a person who really likes nice things, and I love to dress with class. These shoes were real silk shoes, and they were very nice. They also had a gold medal medallion with a lion on the front. Those shoes were all silk, and silk is delicate, and you must take special care of it. If you hit your foot while wearing these silk shoes, your feet would probably snag something sharp that would damage the delicate silk threads. Well, this encounter bothered my religious thinking so much that I did not go and do what Jesus told me in Heaven to do. So some time went by, maybe a few weeks, when I was wearing those shoes, and I accidently snagged the silk while hitting them up against something. Immediately, I felt like Peter when it states in the Bible, *"He remembered the words of Jesus"* (see Matt. 26:75).

At that moment I remembered what Jesus told me in Heaven, and the next day I quickly ran to the store to buy a new pair of those shoes hoping that they were not sold out, and thank God they were not! All I'm trying to say to you is that Christ has taste, and He likes nice things. Later, after trying to find an explanation for this appearance, a good friend of mine brought to my attention how much the Lord likes nice things. The point is that when the Lord told Solomon to build the temple, or when He told Moses to build the tabernacle, He gave them specific details and instructions of what He wanted His temple to look like. He also told them what He wanted inside of it, including how the different furniture pieces should be overlaid with gold, silver, and brass. The Lord has His own style and His own specific personal taste.

Jesus Likes Silk
The Lord Made the Earth in Good Taste

I also heard the testimony of another man who was taken to Heaven and, when he got there, he saw beautiful, majestic mountains with snowcaps and gorgeous, green, luscious valleys at the bottom. He was surprised because he didn't expect to see mountains with snowcaps and valleys in Heaven like there are on earth. So he asked the Lord, "Why are there mountains up here like on earth?" You see, he thought Heaven had a completely different image than earth. And Jesus responded to him, saying, "The earth is the Lord's taste. I created both places, so some of the things you see down there are also up here in Heaven." It is just like looking at several paintings from the same artist, some of the same trends and styles can be seen throughout their different paintings. We must also remember that Jesus was in the beginning with God helping with creation (see John 1:1-3). Silk was one of those creations! When the Lord created the Earth, He put some of the same things He created in Heaven down here. Wow, the earth is the Lord's taste! So the Lord likes some of the things you see here on earth, like silk. He created silk, and He still likes it today.

We Are His Temple and Bride, and He Likes for Us to Be Decorated and Dressed in Silk

Today we are the temple of God, and the Lord has promised to dwell inside of us. Don't you think He likes to decorate His temple still? I saw something interesting in Scripture during Israel's walk with God when the Lord entered into a marriage covenant with them. At this point, they turned away from the

Lord, and He started talking to the nation of Israel like a married man talks to his wife when he is in love with her, by reminding her of all the wonderful things he does for her. One of the things the Lord mentions to Israel is that He covered her in silk when He first found her.

> *I clothed thee also with broidered work...and I covered thee with silk....Thus wast thou decked with gold and silver; and thy raiment was of fine linen, and silk, and broidered work* (Ezekiel 16:10,13).

This Scripture shows the Lord's taste concerning silk in that He wanted His wife to be covered in it. Again, this confirmation shows the Lord has a taste for silk. Now it all makes sense why He called me up to Heaven concerning those silk shoes! After learning this, I was shocked and appalled by the way that I responded in my mind and heart to the Lord when I stood in front of Him face-to-face. He is not a robot or some emotionless, distant God sitting on the throne without His own individual life and personality. I did repent for not obeying Him when He told me to.

THE COUNTENANCE OF YOUR FACE IS IMPORTANT TO HIM.

He Gave Me a Compliment on My Countenance

> *Iron sharpeneth iron; so a man sharpeneth the countenance of his friend* (Proverbs 27:17).

He Knew Me by Face Personally

One night as I was shut away inside the church fasting and praying, the Lord appeared to me, disclosing Himself by words. I was in a deep sleep, sort of like the Bible describes Abraham experiencing (see Gen. 15:12-18). I heard a voice saying, *"Your face is handsome and healthy the way it is."* He said, *"Your face is the perfect size I want it to be."* Then I woke up! At this time I had gained weight and, now in my thirties, weighed more than I had in my entire life. I always thought that somehow I looked more in shape in my teenage years when I was as thin as a tooth pick. Call it vanity or pride, I don't know, but what I did know is that I was thin all the way into my early thirties when I all of a sudden put on a few pounds. I guess my metabolism slowed down. My face filled out, but I didn't get fat! This shocked me that the Lord knew what I was thinking and would encourage me about my face. I had also been going around asking different people if they thought my face was fat or asking, "Do I look fat?" Later, the Lord explained what He meant by this and why He said this to me.

He Loves Your Countenance

You have to understand the Lord is a person, and He can be like a close friend who you can talk to about issues, and who will literally give His feedback to you about it. I asked the Lord, "Why did you comment on my face?" First, He responded, *"To encourage you about your appearance and weight."* Then He said, *"Because I love you, and I know you by face literally."* I had always thought that when the Scripture said, "whom the Lord knew face-to-face," that it didn't refer to a literal reference, but was just a term of intimacy to describe the closeness and friendship between two people (see Exod. 33:11)! But to my surprise, this was not the case. It was surprising to me that the Lord would give me a compliment on my face just as a person would who is a real friend to you. After I read some Scriptures in the Bible, I found out that the Lord commented on how fair and beautiful David's face was.

Now he was ruddy, and withal of a beautiful countenance, and goodly to look to. And the Lord said, Arise, anoint him: for this is he (1 Samuel 16:12).

*And when the Philistine looked about, and saw David, he disdained him: for he was but a youth, **and ruddy, and of a fair countenance*** (1 Samuel 17:42).

We all know that God's Word is His heart and thoughts written on pages. The Lord Himself was complimenting David on his countenance.

HE'S CONCERNED ABOUT YOUR COUNTENANCE.

Throughout history the Lord has always taken notice of the countenance of man. We see this even in the time of Abel and Cain when the Lord commented on Cain's facial expression that had fallen (become disheartened or discouraged) when his sacrifice was not accepted by God. The Lord asked him,

Why is thy countenance fallen? (Genesis 4:6).

Even Jesus in the New Testament said that He did not want us to be of a sad countenance like the hypocritical Pharisees, but instead He wanted us to take care of our face even during our fasting times by washing and anointing it (see Matt. 6:16-17).

HE WANTS TO SEE OUR FACE MORE DESPERATELY THAN WE WANT TO SEE HIS

The Song of Solomon was written symbolically about our intimate, romantic relationship with the Lord, and it speaks about how the Lord wants to see our face, and He compliments us on how lovely our face is to Him.

Let me see thy countenance, let me hear thy voice; for sweet is thy voice, and thy countenance is comely (Song of Solomon 2:14).

You see, in this context, He asks to see our face. You have to understand that He asks to see our face even more desperately than we ask to see His. He wants to know us intimately, more than you could ever realize. When He asks to see our face all we have to do in return is just ask to see His!

What It Means to Be Known by Face

When the Lord says He knows you by name or face, He means literally in the physical realm. This is what Jesus was trying to tell us when He said,

But the very hairs of your head are all numbered (Matthew 10:30).

This verse doesn't say the Lord just knows the count of how many hairs are on your head. No, it's more detailed than that! He said He knows the very *number* of each hair! That's detailed! That means each individual hair has its own number, and He knows when hair number 377 falls out. He cares about every detail of every single strand of your hair. This is confirmed in His statement, *"But there shall not a hair of your head perish"* (Luke 21:18). How awesome!

Wow, if the Lord is so detailed about us that He knows the very number of hairs on our head, how much more interested would He be in our countenance and face, which is even more important? God wants to know you by face. Do you really want this face-to-face relationship with Him? When the Lord knows you by face, then He will also know you by name. Because the face reveals the fullness of who a person is. Everything is revealed from the starting point of the face or countenance of a person. The face is where a person's identity is revealed or changed. This is why God wants face-to-face contact with your life, not just voice-to-voice, or presence-to-presence relationship with you. It is the countenance of a person that tells the motions of his or her whole body. The Bible speaks of how the Lord can know us by name, face, and even speaks with us mouth-to-mouth. If you seek after knowing Him face-to-face, you will also gain a relationship with Him by name and speak to Him mouth-to-mouth.

And there arose not a prophet since in Israel like unto Moses,
whom the Lord knew face to face (Deuteronomy 34:10).

*And the Lord said unto Moses, I will do this thing also that thou hast spoken: for thou hast found grace in My sight, **and I know thee by name** (Exodus 33:17).*

***With him will I speak mouth to mouth,** even apparently, and not in dark speeches; and the similitude of the Lord shall he behold (Numbers 12:8).*

The Lord had to have some kind of face-to-face contact with Moses because the mouth is an element of the face. But the Bible records most frequently that the Lord knew Moses face-to-face, even at the end of his life! This was phenomenal back in the Old Testament, considering that we were limited in our relationship with the Lord because of sin and our fallen nature. But since Jesus has dealt with the issue of sin, we are now free to enjoy a relationship face-to-face with Jesus Christ. We can literally see Jesus face-to-face. I know I have! Many in the Bible literally saw Jesus face-to-face. This is what Paul meant when he said,

*For now we see through a glass, darkly; **but then face to face:** now I know in part; but then shall I know even as also I am known (1 Corinthians 13:12).*

Paul was saying here that the Lord knew Him face-to-face. It is one thing for the Lord to know you face-to-face, but it's another thing for you to know Him face-to-face. It's special for you to have knowledge of His countenance in an intimate way like He knows yours. From this experience, I can honestly say that the Lord knows me face-to-face. My pursuit is to know Him face-to-face as well.

THOU ART THE HEALTH
OF MY COUNTENANCE

After Jesus visited me and encouraged me about my countenance, He appeared again the very next night. I was asleep on the church floor when I suddenly heard His still, gentle voice saying, *"An apple will help heal the skin around your nose, and prevent it from peeling and shedding. Apples heal the skin on your face."* Then His voice left as soon as it came. There was a still silence in the atmosphere that I could feel even though I was sleep! He was gone, but the atmosphere where He had just been was filled with the essence of peace and glory from Him walking in.

This time I did not see Him. I just heard Him! Then I suddenly awoke. Again He was talking to me about my face. My nose had always shed skin and peeled throughout the years, but when I started eating apples like the Lord said, it healed, and the peeling went away. I didn't totally understand, but as I was studying God's Word, I came across the Scripture where David said,

> *Why art thou cast down, O my soul? and why art thou disquieted within me? hope thou in God: for I shall yet praise Him, who is the health of my countenance, and my God* (Psalm 42:11).

I thought, *"How awesome!"* When the Lord knows you face-to-face, He is literally concerned about the health of your physical countenance. I started eating apples from that time forward, maybe not as much as I should have, but more than I had been eating them! My friend, the Lord also loves your countenance! He wants to "know" (to gain knowledge through an intimate experience by manifestation with Him) you face-to-face. Are you willing?

The Messiah Is Jewish
He Still Practices His Jewish Culture and Heritage

In this next visitation that I'm about to describe, I learned something fascinating about Jesus. I learned that He still practices His Jewish lifestyle and culture. You must understand that it was God the Father who chose Israel to be the nation that would be unique to Him, before we as the Gentiles were chosen to be a part of God's family in the New Testament. Because many of us don't understand Jewish culture, we don't recognize the significance of why the Lord taught the Jews certain lifestyles and behaviors. God chose the Jewish culture to reveal and express His lifestyle, ways, and actions to all nations in the earth during the time of the Old Testament. Jesus, who was Jewish, was the last prophet and representative to express this image and nature of God before the Jewish culture rejected Him. He then delivered over His kingdom to a new people (see Matt. 21:43).

Christians Have a Rich Heritage in Judaism

Our problem is that as the Body of Christ, we haven't studied our Jewish roots, which leaves us ignorant and unaware of a lot of Jesus' expressions, manners, customs, and ways. This is what happened to me. My views of who Jesus is were limited in many respects. This one visitation changed all of this. From this particular face-to-face visitation, I saw how much I still didn't know Jesus. This all happened one day when a staff member came to tell me that Jesus had appeared to her that night and gave her a message for the ministry. It is so amazing to me to see how Jesus visits my whole staff on a face-to-face basis. Everyone, including the children, is having these face-to-face appearances from the Lord.

Jesus Pronounces Victory in an Appearance

While she was sleeping, Jesus came to her in a dream. She described how He had on a white robe and how she wanted to ask Him a question. Jesus turned to her and kneeled in front of her while saying these words concerning our ministry, *"I have given you the victory."* The ministry had been under an attack, so I understood why Jesus was saying this. When she explained to me how He kneeled in front of her, I had serious problems with that, and I even expressed this to her! I thought, "Wait a minute. Jesus does not have to bow, nor does it say He bows to us." The Scripture does record that we will, with everyone else, bow our knees at the mention of His name! I didn't understand this part of the visitation because of my ignorance of the Jewish culture and practices and because of my religious and westernized mind-set. I asked the Lord about it. One day, a few weeks after this woman had this face-to-face encounter with the Lord, I was doing my daily studying of God's Word and His presence in the room was so wonderful! When all of a sudden, I came across a Hebrew word that opened up this whole visitation to me. I came across the Hebrew word *barak.*

REMEMBER YOUR JEWISH ROOTS.

Barak is the Hebrew word which means "to bless."[6] It means to kneel and bless God or man as an act of adoration! Wow! When my eyes moved on the page to this word, the Holy Spirit opened up my understanding to this whole visitation. At that moment, I felt the power of God go through me, and Glory filled my room. I used to think that the word for bless in the New Testament meant what we in America mean by blessing someone. I thought it meant to bless those who curse you as Matthew 5:44 says to do.

I thought it meant to do something good for them. So I would go out and buy a present or gift for those who spoke evil against me. I found out later that I was totally wrong because I was not following the instructions that Jesus gave us when we are cursed by another. The word *curse* in this context also means to speak evil about someone! I looked up that word *bless* in the New Testament, and it means "to speak well of," and, when I saw this, I realized I was wrong. I had been taught by American Christians that to bless someone was to go out and buy or do something good for them. This is not what Jesus was talking about; He was saying to speak well of those who are cursing you. I also saw that this was more difficult to do than just going and buying them a gift because it is easier to give something, and I am generous by nature. So Jesus was basically saying that when we are under an attack from someone who is speaking evil of us, we in turn are supposed to do the opposite by speaking well of them.

Jesus said that this is the nature of the children of God. I understood this much about the word *bless* by studying it in the Greek, but I hadn't yet studied the Hebrew word for bless. So when I saw what this meant, I realized that Jesus was speaking well over us, and by physically kneeling, He was living His own Word. He was "baraking" us. Then I saw the glorious revelation that Jesus still practices His Hebraic customs and culture that the Lord commanded the Jewish nation. Wow! Jesus is Jewish. He lives by His own words and the words of His Father!

Jesus Still Talks About His Hometown of Nazareth

He Does Not Forget Where God Brought Him From

And He said unto me, I am Jesus of Nazareth (Acts 22:8).

...denying the Lord that bought them (2 Peter 2:1).

Even though Jesus has been given a name that is above every name, He still does not forget where God the Father brought Him from. The Bible talks about those who will deny the Lord. Jesus still doesn't deny the place of His hometown or where the Lord God brought Him from. When He appeared to Paul on the road to Damascus, He mentioned His personal hometown when Paul asked Him who He was.

And I fell unto the ground, and heard a voice saying unto me, Saul, Saul, why persecutest thou Me? And I answered, Who art Thou, Lord? And He said unto me, I am Jesus of Nazareth, whom thou persecutest (Acts 22:7-8).

As the Son of Man, Jesus came through the Jewish lineage. As the Son of God, He carried the divine nature of God. He was a Jew as much as He was the Divine Son of God. We must understand this!

He's a Man of Few Words

I always wondered when Jesus appeared to me why the visitations were short and why He only spoke very few words, causing them to last only moments. When the Lord appears to you who are reading this book, like He is going to do, you will notice that His words are few and short. You will not find when He comes to you in these appearances that Jesus constantly talks like some people who talk too much. Instead, He talks by sentences, statements, or by explanations to make a point. From what I have seen, being face-to-face with Jesus personally, He talked more when He walked the earth over two thousand years ago than He does now to us. He even made this point that He would not speak much to us after He left this earth.

Hereafter I will not talk much with you: for the prince of this world cometh, and hath nothing in Me (John 14:30).

Jesus says that He would be limited in how much He would talk to His disciples after this point compared to how much He had talked to them before. This goes for us too. One of Jesus' reasons for not talking as much was that satan was about to come against Jesus, which we saw take place during His trial, persecution, and crucifixion. He limited His words during that period—going to the slaughter mute—and not opening His mouth. Another reason is because this is His personality as a meek person. Meek people do not talk a lot unnecessarily; they are people of few words and are very quiet about things when necessary. Jesus is this way. He is a Man of few words. The Bible speaks that we should let our words be few as well (see Eccles. 5:2). It also tells us in God's Word that in the multitude of words (or when we talk too much), sin is evidently very present in our conversation.

In the multitude of words there wanteth not sin: but he that refraineth his lips is wise (Proverbs 10:19).

It also says in James that we should be quick to hear and slow to speak (see James 1:19). Jesus is the *Word* of God Himself, and the written Word of God (the Bible) admonishes us to let our words be few. Well, Jesus is this Word personified. His personality expresses what is written in the Bible, and I have witnessed this personally.

ENDNOTES

1. Benny Hinn, *The Anointing* (Nashville, TN: Thomas Nelson, Inc., 1997).

2. "Shalat": see http://www.studylight.org/lex/heb/view.cgi?number=07980.

3. "Sebastos": see http://www.studylight.org/lex/grk/view.cgi?number=4575.

4. *Merriam-Webster's Collegiate Dictionary*, *11th ed.*, s.v. "Imperial."

5. Mark Altrogge, "I Stand in Awe"; see http://www.ccli. com/WorshipResources/SongStories.cfm?itemID=9.

6. "Barak": see http://www.studylight.org/lex/heb/view. cgi?number=01288.

He Appears and Shows Me the Most Important Thing About Him: His Heart

He Appears and Shows Me the Most Important Thing About Him: His Heart

The Lamb King

His Nature—The Lion and the Lamb

I had another face-to-face encounter with Jesus during my first year in college after I left home. I had graduated from high school and was off to Charleston, South Carolina. Charleston is a beautiful place! I really enjoyed the beautiful moss trees and Atlantic Ocean during my stay there. At this time in my walk with the Lord, I was really fascinated by the four beasts that surrounded God's throne in Ezekiel chapter 1. As I studied these beasts, the Scripture astounded me as it described their appearance and power. As a young Christian, I made a lot of immature and foolish mistakes by getting distracted by angels rather than the presence of the Lord. I desired and asked the Lord to show me these four angelic beasts. I wanted to see them like I had seen the Lord. Like so many other Christians, I began to become fascinated with these angelic creatures. The visitation that I am about to explain to you caused me to understand that God was doing something more special in my life beyond seeing angels. I have seen so many immature Christians and, sad to say, even those who are mature, focus more on angelic appearances than appearances from the Lord. By this they are missing the main focus and the greatest experience of all time! The Lord Himself is the greatest experience for all eternity. I also noticed in Scripture a fabulous point in Moses' life when God told him that He would send an angel to lead and guide the Israelites into the place that He had promised (see Exod. 23:20). Moses loved the Lord so intensely, and had such a close relationship with God that, out of hunger, he refused to enter the Promised Land if God wouldn't go with them (see Exod. 33:12-17). Wow! How many of us would have settled for the angels that God would send instead of insisting that God come with us, Moses said, *"If Thy presence go not with me, carry us not up hence"* (Exod. 33:15). So Moses' life was fully based on his relationship with God's presence more than the presence of angels. We thank God for the angels and what they are called to do by ministering to our lives and to those in our families by helping to bring them into salvation in the Kingdom of God.

Are they not all ministering spirits, sent forth to minister for them who shall be heirs of salvation? (Hebrews 1:14).

What I'm saying here is that their presence cannot be compared to the Lord's presence. We should focus more on the Lord than His angels. After praying to see those powerful creatures, Jesus showed up in a dream Himself instead!

The Visitation—He Comes Again
The Lion of Judah-Lamb King Appearance

When I fell fast asleep, I was immediately in a dream. In this dream, I was standing in the middle of the street, and I saw into Heaven. In front of me, I saw a temple sitting in the Heavens; the doors of the temple opened suddenly, and there He was (see Rev. 11:19). Again, He was standing in front of me, but this time He was more regal and magnificent than ever before, and in a different form than I had ever seen Him in. The Bible mentions that the Lord has appeared in different forms.

After that He appeared in another form unto two of them (Mark 16:12).

In this dream I saw Him as the Lion of the tribe of Judah that is mentioned in Revelation 5:5. There stood Jesus, and His face was as a lion, a real lion, and it was pure gold, but He was alive! He had the most beautiful golden lion mane around His neck. His face was brilliant and astounding. I was captivated. I knew it was Jesus, but I had never seen Him in this awesome and magnificent form. The rest of His body was as a normal man from His neck down. He also had on a beautiful, light-blue garment that I had never ever seen Him wearing before. In almost every other visitation, He had worn a beautiful white robe, but in this appearance He had on a light-blue garment that looked like a gown. The Bible refers to a garment of salvation and to a robe of righteousness (see Isa. 61:10). There is a difference between a gown and a robe. The most striking thing about Him in this appearance was that His face was pure gold, in the form of a lion. His pure gold face could never have been mistaken as a statue—I knew He was living! He stood in front of Heaven's doors with His gold lion-face, and with the garments on His body in a man's form. The next thing I noticed were His arms and hands stretched out in front of Him with a little book in the palm of His right hand. I had read about this in Revelation 5:5-7, but didn't understand what those passages of Scriptures meant as a young Christian. Nonetheless, in time I fully came to understand the symbolism and revelation of this appearance of Jesus during this dream. Understand that Jesus can appear to you in dreams.

When Jesus Appears to You in Your Sleep

The dream realm is just as real and important as the physical realm. In these dreams, there may be symbolism, proverb phrases, and parabolic scenes that carry messages in themselves. The point is that the dream realm is just as real as the physical realm, no matter how many symbols are in the dream that you don't understand. We see that Solomon's life is a testimony of this. The Bible says in First Kings 3:5 that the Lord *appeared* to Solomon by night in a dream and told him he had the opportunity to ask the Lord "whatsoever he willed." Solomon asked for wisdom, and we see that this wisdom was given to him, and that it manifested openly in his life and became real in the physical realm. The Scriptures state, *"And Solomon awoke; and, behold, it was a dream"* (1 Kings 3:15). Dreams from God are important because they reveal future and present events that will manifest in the physical realm. We know that Solomon was the wisest man in the world, but this wisdom that he received was imparted to him from God through a dream.

In this dream, as I saw the Lord standing there with His lion face, another being ran past me in a human form, and I knew it was satan. As he ran past me, he bumped into me, and I asked him, "Why are you running?" Then he replied to me, "Jesus the lion chased me through the temple to get me out. But because He was so big, He transformed into the Lamb so that He could fit through the archways and doors of the temple." Jesus visited me in this unusual way soon after my salvation. This visitation occured about eight to ten months after I had initially come to the Lord. I did not understand the significance of this vision at that time, but I discovered why he revealed Himself to me as both the Lion and the Lamb later.

From this experience God wanted me to learn and understand two things:

1.) He did not want me distracted from this special face-to-face relationship with Him—not even distracted by angels! This was His focus for my life at the time even though I did not understand it fully.

2.) I didn't understand it at the time, but Jesus was trying to teach me His heart of meekness and humility in the first season of my relationship with Him. Meekness and humility are a top priority with Him as the Bible affirms.

It has taken me 15 years to articulate this revelation drawn from this face-to-face experience with Jesus. You see, when we first come to Him, many saints like myself have missed His priorities as we begin to learn about Him. One of the first instructions

He gives us is to learn of Him through considering His heart of meekness and lowliness. He says,

Come unto Me... Take My yoke upon you, and learn of Me; for I am meek and lowly in heart (Matthew 11:28-29).

Jesus was referring us back to Himself here. He wanted us to learn about Him, and then in the next breath, He gives us the key to learning about Him when He says about Himself, *"For I am meek and lowly in heart."* The Lord at this time was trying to teach me His nature and the wisdom of meekness and lowliness as the Lamb, not just the Lion. It wasn't until years later that I understood I had made a grave error in focusing on many other things about the Lord rather than on His heart. It cost me many mistakes, much time, and needless pain. I could have been much farther today if I had understood Jesus' purpose for telling us to study and learn this part of His nature when first coming to Him. When you are a young Christian, you want to learn and study other things about Jesus that seem more exciting instead of focusing on His heart. Subjects about Him like meekness and humility are boring to the fleshly man. Our flesh is more alive than anything when we initially get saved, and this is the reason we gravitate after the seemingly more sensational and exciting things of the Lord.

His Heart: Meekness and Humility
Learning the First Priority About Jesus

I didn't understand the revelation that Jesus was showing me until years later. His nature as the Lion is too big at times, when driving the enemy out of a place, to bring deliverance. Sometimes it takes His Lamb-like nature, power, and strength to remove a demonic influence. I didn't get the hint that it was not the lion nature that He was trying to get me to focus on, but His nature as the Lamb. Years later, the Lord gave me an important lesson about what He was actually trying to accomplish in this visitation. You have to understand that when we see Him, the appearance should change us in some way to become more like Him. At that stage in my life, I was immature and didn't catch on. This was the next major physical face-to-face encounter that I had with him after my initial conversion. Then it all became clear when Jesus, by His Spirit, explained to me why He allowed this visitation to be the next significant appearance I had. When Jesus extended the invitation for us to come to Him in Matthew 11:28, He promises to give our souls rest as we come to Him. After getting saved, one of the first things Jesus tells us to do is to take His yoke upon us and learn of Him (see Matt. 11:29).

Then He says the most powerful statement in the universe, *"Learn of Me* [or about who I am] *for I am meek and lowly in heart"* (Matt. 11:29). Right here, Jesus gives all of us an invitation to learn who He really is as a person. Most of us, myself included, missed this principle, in the beginning of our conversion. We go through this long pursuit of trying to know Him and find out who God is and don't realize that Jesus is saying to start here. He was basically saying to me, *"If you want to learn who I am, and know Me, I'll give you the first two clues of the foundation of My whole life. Start learning these first: I am meek and lowly in heart."* I've learned that if you really want to know a person, you must know their heart. The heart reveals the character, nature, and ways of the person. Also, knowing a person's heart gives you understanding about them and answers the questions you have about why they do things the way they do them.

Understanding His Priorities

> ### YOU WILL WASTE TIME
> ### IF YOU DON'T DO IT HIS WAY.

I lamented, cried, and wept because I had walked with the Lord and missed studying and learning the very thing that He tells us to prioritize learning about. Most of us, when we initially come to Him, don't take the right process in learning who He is as a meek and lowly hearted person, and this gets us into so much trouble. As a matter of fact, I believe that every pastor should make it a requirement in their church for new converts to learn and study the meek and humble heart of Jesus as He tells us to do. We'd rather start learning of Him as the anointed one, or about His anointing, power, gifts, and prosperity. We study what interests us about Jesus. This is wrong, according to His standards, and oh, how I saw and learned this the hard way. I was so interested in the supernatural aspects of His character. Looking back, I know that studying His meekness or humility would have been boring to me. I wanted to know about what I thought was more exciting about Him. When He appeared to me, I wanted the relationship with Him beyond the gifts and the anointing, and I sought Him. I didn't understand that in this visitation He was trying to take me down the proper path, and establish His learning priorities in me so that I could really know Him. Because I learned this later in life, I realized that even though we enjoyed years of wonderful fellowship and friendship, I still didn't know who He was. Let me make this point. Knowing Him is not determined by how many face-to-face appearances Jesus gives you. The appearances do not mean you really know Him as a person. You may see Him face-to-face and learn things about Him, which is good. He may come to you in person and give you great experiences with Him, but all of this is still shallow until you learn His heart! Learning in depth the first two foundational parts of His makeup and personality, meekness and humility, are the first keys to knowing Him as a person. It's when you learn this part of His heart that you will really understand intimately who He really is, His ways, and why He does things the way He does them! This helps us to understand why He responds and acts in the manner He does, even when He appears to you. After I learned this lesson, I looked back over all the encounters I had with Him and evaluated His every move and action, and found it linked with the character of His heart—meekness and humility.

Are Your Priorities Aligned With His in This Area?

This sounds so simple, and yet the Lord told me that 98 percent of His people miss this revelation about Him. After I learned about His heart, the Gospels that described Jesus' actions and lifestyle became clear to me. The reasons He taught the way He taught and lived the way He lived became clear to me. I cried and wept saying, "Lord, forgive me for wasting so much time in my walk with You even though You were giving me all these wonderful trips to Heaven and glorious appearances from You." I had seen the Lord many times by the time that I understood the depth of the heart of meekness and lowliness. You see, I thought in the beginning that I knew, but I didn't. Most of the time we assume we know things about the Lord when we really don't. I thought, *"How could I have seen Him so many times and missed this?"* I even saw this meek character in His nature when He would appear, but couldn't articulate it. Now today I rejoice, as the Lord said in Scripture, *"But let him that glorieth glory in this, that he understandeth and knoweth Me"* (Jer. 9:24).

THE KINGDOM IS BUILT ON THE HEART OF THE KING

Jesus said, *"Seek ye first the kingdom of God, and His righteousness; and all these things shall be added unto you"* (see Matt. 6:33). Translated, this means seek first the King, and then His domain. The Kingdom is built on the heart of the King. You can't really understand the message of the Kingdom of God without first understanding its King. This is where we are lacking in America. We are trying to study and learn what the Kingdom of God is, but don't know the King. You cannot study Jesus' Kingdom alone. This is not what the Lord meant. You must study Heaven's King in conjunction with His Kingdom, and then His message on His Kingdom will become clear to you. Understanding the heart of the King is understanding Him. Understanding Him is understanding His full message on the Kingdom of God that He preached. This is why Jesus gave Peter the premier keys of His Kingdom above all the other disciples. Peter was given the revelation of who Jesus was as the Son of God and who He was as King. After He had this revelation from the Father, the Lord then said to him,

> *But whom say ye that I am? And Simon Peter answered and said, Thou art the Christ, the Son of the Living God. And Jesus answered and said unto him, Blessed art thou, Simon Bar-jona: for flesh and blood hath not revealed it unto thee, but My Father which is in Heaven. And I say also unto thee, that thou art Peter, and **upon this rock I will build My church;** and the gates of hell shall not prevail against it. And I will give unto thee the keys of the king-dom of heaven: and whatsoever thou shalt bind on earth shall be bound in Heaven: and whatsoever thou shalt loose on earth shall be loosed in Heaven* (Matthew 16:15-19).

You see, Peter was given the keys of the kingdom *after* He understood who Jesus was. They weren't given to Him before this time! Wow! What revelation! This is the point: you can't even began to understand the Lord's Kingdom or the message of it until you have a revelation of who the King, Messiah, and Son of God is! Amazingly, once you understand the total revelation of who Jesus is, you too will hold the keys, and hell or its gates of authority will not be able to prevail against you!

THE GATES OF HELL WILL NOT BE
ABLE TO PREVAIL AGAINST THE REVELATION
OF JESUS CHRIST IN YOUR LIFE.

This is one of the main reasons this subject of knowing Jesus face-to-face is important—the gates or authorities of hell will not be able to prevail against you or your life. When you learn about Jesus like this, hell and its authorities will only be used as training or practice to build your strength. The point is, when you have a revelation about who Jesus is, you will prevail against satanic authorities and their strategies. Hell will not be able to prevail against you. Instead, you will prevail and have victory with this relationship!

The Lamb

Learning What He Is Really Like at Heart

If you are going to experience the depths of Jesus Christ and understand with an intimate knowledge who He is, you must learn His heart. I've heard of many of God's servants who have had multiple visitations, face-to-face appearances, and experiences from the Lord and think they know him, but in reality they are acquainted with Him but do not really know Him intimately. Some may think that because they have had visitations, they really know Him, but according to Scripture and truth, this is not true. They are mistaking an intimate experience from Jesus for an intimate understanding and knowledge of Jesus. There's a difference! The Lord's whole purpose for us is to get an understanding of who He is in person and not just an experience of what He's like or how He looks. Like the Bible says, I will sing with the understanding and I will speak with the understanding that all may be edified (see 1 Cor. 14:15-19). We must also have an intimate experience with the understanding of who He is as a person. Paul says, *"I count all things but loss for the excellency of the knowledge of Christ Jesus my Lord…that I may win Christ"* (Phil. 3:8).

Gaining the Excellency of the Knowledge of Christ

Notice that Paul didn't say he counts all things but loss just for the *knowledge* of Christ, but for the *excellency* of the knowledge (see Phil. 3:7-10). In other words, Jesus can start initially giving you all these experiences and allowing you to walk with Him for years without revealing to you who He really is as a person. I said years later, "Lord, why would you give us all these experiences and not tell us this truth about who You are in person and at heart?" Then He said to me, *"David, it is your job to learn of Me! The condition and command I gave you when coming to Me was to learn about Me and My heart. I hinted and referred to Myself as being meek and lowly of heart. You failed to see this invitation from Me. I hinted to you to learn about Me as I have done to so many others among My greatest servants and friends. I am glad you are learning about Me now."* You see His heart reveals His face. It's not until you look at Jesus' heart that you can know, understand, or interpret His face and the depths of the expression in it.

Knowing His heart reveals His whole life, nature, and whereabouts! The heart reveals the face, actions, ways, decisive plans, strategies, and decisions of a person. It is true when the Scripture says that out of the heart *"are the issues of life"* (Prov. 4:23). Jesus' life flows from His heart, and His heart is meek and lowly. Everything Jesus says and does comes out of His heart. If you are going to understand and know Jesus, you have to understand the depth of His meekness and lowliness. Also, to know the Lord's voice and understand His speech, parables, and riddles of words requires that you know His heart (see John 8:43). For Jesus Himself gave us this key saying, *"Out of the abundance of the heart the mouth speaketh"* (Matt. 12:34). If you can understand His speech, voice, and the reasons why He talks the way the He does (which is softly, gently, and mildly), it's because you also know His heart. This meek and lowly heart explains why His voice is soft and still like His Father's (see 1 Kings 19:12).

Understanding His Heart Helps Explain His Actions and Ways

The nature of your heart determines the decisions and issues that flow forth from your heart. God lives His Word. He's placed His Word above His name (see Ps. 138:2). Jesus was trying to get us to see that *"You will know and understand Me only if you can understand My heart."* There was a young man who asked me, "Why does God stay invisible to us most of the time while we are here on earth?" You must understand that a person acts or does things as a result of the issues that flow out of his or her heart. I answered him from this standpoint. The Father and Jesus do everything from the nature and issues of their heart. He hides because He is meek. Meekness is the hidden man of the heart. Meekness has to do with being silent, quiet, and hidden (see 1 Pet. 3:4). Meekness comes from the Greek word *praus* which means, "To be gentle or mild mannered."[1] This is the way Jesus is. God doesn't let us see Him every day because of the hidden nature of His heart. His decision to be this way emerges from the issues flowing from His heart. If you do not first learn or understand the foundation of Jesus' heart of meekness and lowliness, you will fail in knowing the whole person of Jesus Christ (see Matt. 11:29)!

Jesus can also be bold, austere, and firm as when He drove the people who were doing wrong out of the temple. He's not like that all of the time, nor is this His normal, consistent personality or nature. As a meek person, He's mild and easy going. He's very gentle and tender, and the look on His face expresses the same consistency of meekness and lowliness in His heart. He does not have a hard or harsh look on His face; instead, there's a softness and tenderness in His eyes when He looks at you. At other times, His eyes can be a flame of fire. I know this because I've seen the exact same facial expression when He has appeared to me. I was unbalanced. I knew Him as the Lion, but didn't know Him as the Lamb.

Jesus Is a Meek Person

The Behavior of a Meek Person

Have you ever noticed that when you are around people who are very meek you have to basically draw them out, and ask them questions to get them to communicate with you? This is what you must understand about Jesus. He does not talk a lot, and He's short in His speech (see John 14:30). Meek people have different reasons for being quiet concerning various topics, as Jesus explains in John 16:12. He said, *"I have yet many things to say unto you, but ye cannot bear them now."* Meek people exercise gentleness through being quiet when they know that what they may say could be burdensome to the person at that moment.

He Is Considerate

This brings me to another one of the characteristics of the nature of meekness and a person who has this type of disposition.

Jesus spoke of desiring to give others rest. The nature and the characteristic of a meek person is a restful experience. This means they are not burdensome, harsh, or overbearing. They do not say things that people can't bear at that moment. Jesus spoke of His fellowship being easy. It's easy being around meek people because they give you a restful experience. This characterizes the nature of Jesus. He gives us a restful experience in all that we do when we are yoked with Him. When life becomes burdensome, stressful, and overbearing, you are not walking in His way. How beautiful! I said all of these things to bring you to one point, and that is that you may learn how to discern God's voice when He speaks to you in dreams.

His Voice

His Gentle Whisper

If you really want to accurately interpret what the Lord is saying to you, it is very important that you understand His nature, because His voice speaks from the same character of His heart. It is important to realize that Jesus has already told us what His heart is like when He told us that He's meek and lowly in heart. Jesus Himself said that people speak from their heart. This establishes the point that the Lord's voice is meek and lowly in character. Therefore, His voice reflects His heart. Those who are lowly and humble of heart choose to act in small ways. There is humility in their character, in their conduct, and in the way they do things.

The Bible also says that the Lord's voice is still, meaning that there is a quietness and stillness in His voice. *This could mean that although the Lord is saying something to you, there is also a lot that He is not saying to you.* In order to understand the nature of His voice and interpret what He is saying in dreams, you must understand who He is, and how He operates as a meek and humble person. Again, meekness speaks of a person being quiet, still, peaceful, and silent with a pure "stealth" motive in their actions. Humility, on the other hand, which is different from meekness, speaks of a person not necessarily *being* small, but *acting* in a small and simple manner. It speaks of a person with great modesty, regardless of whether his or her rank is great. It speaks of a person's attitude displaying the behavior of voluntarily being least or last. Making a conscious decision to display this type of attitude is not a display of false humility, or because someone is struggling against pride. On the contrary, this is a way of life for meek people.

If you want to definitely hear God's voice and really understand what He is saying, you must understand what meekness and humility are. Jesus mentioned that the abundance of the heart flows out of our mouths. First we must establish the fact that the heart of Jesus is also the heart of God the Father. It says in Hebrews 1:3 that Jesus was the express image of the Father. This shows us that God's heart and voice are meek and humble. Meekness in the Bible means having a hidden and quiet personality. The behavior of a meek person is described in First Peter 3:4 as a person who chooses to hold back from saying too much. Therefore, demonstrating a quiet spirit is great wisdom according to Proverbs 29:11.

He Is a Perfect Gentleman

A meek person hides their nature without trying to be deceptive. They are characterized by gentleness. They do not volunteer excessive information about themselves as a form of

165

courtesy, respect, and honor. Jesus is a perfect gentleman because He is meek. Remember, the Greek word for meekness is *praus* which means to be soft, and to exercise gentleness in behavior, actions, and words when dealing with others.

Meek people are soft in nature, and they exercise great restraint in saying things that could be helpful in another's life. Meekness embodies integrity, and those who are meek allow others to pursue them, seeking out further details on their own. Being a gentleman is also being gentle in how much information you give another. If they don't ask, meekness simply does not volunteer the information. This is how Jesus is. There are a lot of things that He would say to us, but because of His meek nature, He does not volunteer the information until He is asked or sought. This type of behavior in the earlier days of my walk with God frustrated me because I did not understand what this was, and did not recognize that it was the character of God. I didn't realize how beautiful His personality is.

Because I have such an outgoing and aggressive nature, this behavior irritated me when I saw silent people who had a spirit of meekness about them. I felt like they were too quiet, and that they should speak more often.

This revelation of meekness opened my eyes to discern the *Lord working in the most hidden matters and speaking in some of the quietest ways that I had not recognized in the past.* This revelation helped me interpret dreams on a whole new level and in a whole new light. It caused me to hear not only what God was saying, but also what *He* was *not saying. I heard what the Lord didn't say in His quietness. This is the strange thing about meekness.* There is a voice and a message even in the quietness.

To give you a good example of this, I remember a story that Kenneth Hagin wrote about in his book called *Plans, Purposes, and Pursuits.*[2] I would like to share it with you to confirm this truth. Dad Hagin shared that during one season of his life the Spirit of the Lord prompted him to start praying for God's plan, purpose, and pursuit for his life and ministry. By this time in his life, he had pastored for somewhere between 15 to 20 years. *After praying this prayer, he had a face-to-face visitation from the Lord Jesus Christ.* During this visitation, Jesus began to talk to him about His plans and purposes for his life. In this visitation, Jesus responded to what he had been asking God and praying for. Dad Hagin also shared in his book that during this face-to-face visitation from Jesus, the Lord told him that he had pastored 15 to 20 years outside of His will, and that He was never called to be a pastor, but a prophet and a teacher. He asked Jesus, "Why didn't you tell me before now that I was pastoring outside of Your will for these many years? Why did You let me go on like this for this long?" Jesus replied to him saying, *"Because you never asked."*

This amazed me when I read this story because it showed me that Jesus will be silent about a lot of things that you are doing, even when those things are good works, until you voluntarily ask Him what His will is. This is how meek people are; they are very quiet about things and will not volunteer certain information until they are asked to do so. This is what you call gentleness. This is being a gentleman. Wow, Jesus is a perfect gentleman!

OUR KING COMES TO US IN MEEKNESS.

His Meek and Lowly Heart Is His Personality
The Purpose of First Learning About His Meek and Lowly Heart

It took me years to understand why Jesus wanted us to study His heart when we initially come to Him. This revelation became clear to me after the Lord taught me His heart. Jesus' heart is the foundation for why He does things the way He does them. The heart is known as the soil of a man's life (see Matt. 13:1-23). Jesus described several kinds of soil. Most of the soils that He talked about were hardened and hindered in a way that made it difficult for the Word of God to grow properly and produce the right type of fruit in an individual's life. Jesus mentioned that the parable of the sower was the parable of all parables. He also said to His disciples (and this also includes us) that if we didn't come to understand the full knowledge of this parable that we would not come to the full knowledge of any of His other parables (see Mark 4:13). The reason is that the soil represents the condition of a man's heart.

If the condition of the man's heart is not soft and gentle, allowing seeds to be easily sown into it, and is instead hard, the right type of fruit will not grown in a man's life. The words that Jesus uses to describe a good heart are the same words that describe meekness. The condition of our heart means everything! Jesus was trying to teach us that the good ground in the parable correlates to the condition of His heart, which is meek, soft, tender, mild, and lowly.

He wanted us to study His heart first so that we would have the right foundation to begin with. He wanted this so that His Word would take root in the right soil which would cause us to produce great fruit. Unfortunately, we come to the Lord after getting saved and don't focus on getting Jesus' heart. This causes us to not see how stony our hearts really are. We end up going through our Christian walk, hearing the Word of God, and producing little fruit or none at all because we didn't understand that we should be pursuing a soft heart. He was basically telling us, *"Listen! Learn about My heart and study it. This is the type of heart you need to develop in order to be successful with Me."* This is why I made so many mistakes over the years. I didn't have to, but I did because I didn't understand this truth. Jesus was trying to get this truth through to me, but I missed the whole revelation of the meekness of the Lamb.

MEEKNESS IS HIS STRATEGY AGAINST SATAN.

The Hidden Mystery of Wisdom in God—Meekness
The Lamb—The Meek King

He was trying to teach me deliverance in this face-to-face visitation. Casting or driving satan out is not always accomplished with the authority and boldness of the Lion, but with the wisdom of the Lamb. The Lion conquers, but the Lamb rules. We are more than conquerors. This is what He was trying to reveal to me in this visitation. We are not only to be bold as conquering lions, but we are to understand the moments of divine warfare that require the strategy, softness, and meekness in the Lamb's powerful nature! He was showing me His power as the Lamb of God in this visitation, but it was hidden. All I saw were His Lion attributes, and I missed the revelation of His Lamb attributes, which are just as powerful. This Scripture began to resound loudly with understanding within me: *"Worthy is the Lamb that was slain to receive power, and riches, and wisdom, and strength, and honour, and glory, and blessing"* (see Rev. 5:12). Notice that it is the sacrificial Lamb, not the Lion, who is praised as worthy in this verse.

The Mystery of His Heart: Meekness, Humility, and Lowliness

When Jesus died on the cross, He was using the hidden wisdom of God, meekness, to finish the work. The mystery and hidden wisdom of God is meekness and lowliness as a Lamb. His strategy was to win the souls of men by dying on the cross as the Lamb. His death at the cross was the winning blow against principalities. In His wisdom, God strategically used the cross to defeat satan's power.

Jesus Defeated satan at the Cross With Meekness

This is what the Lord was trying to teach me through this visitation. He was showing me how it's not always the Lion-likeness of His nature that accomplishes the full deliverance against satan. It is His strategy against satan as the Lamb that instead brings victory. He went to the cross as a silent Lamb; He didn't say anything in His own defense when He was crucified at Calvary. This was not defeat, but it was the hidden wisdom of God that strategically accomplished deliverance for mankind. If the princes of this world knew that Jesus' cross on

Calvary would be their undoing, they would have never crucified the Lord of glory.

> *But we speak the **wisdom of God in a mystery**, even the hidden wisdom, which God ordained before the world unto our glory: which none of the princes of this world knew: for had they known it, **they would not have crucified the Lord of glory*** (1 Corinthians 2:7-8).

To confirm this, the Bible says that Jesus' meekness in bearing the cross spoiled principalities and powers by openly triumphing over them with the cross:

> *Blotting out the handwriting of ordinances that was against us, which was contrary to us, and took it out of the way, **nailing it to His cross; and having spoiled principalities and powers, He made a shew of them openly, triumphing over them in it*** (Colossians 2:14-15).

He Showed His Work in the Earth as the Wise and Meek Lamb of God

> *Let him shew out of a good conversation his works with meekness of wisdom* (James 3:13).

This is how Jesus did His work—with the wisdom of meekness. Jesus possessed and displayed qualities of meekness during His trial, persecution, and crucifixion, by being silent and not opening His mouth. It took power to do this. This was the power of the Lamb—to go in with a gentle strategy to endure incomprehensible pain, but accomplish the greatest deliverance of all time! This is why Jesus always comes to us meek and lowly. Our

King comes to us in meekness. That's the strategy of Heaven, to be sent forth as the Lamb and not as the Lion. This is how God sent Jesus, and this is how Jesus sends us as His disciples and servants. He said, *"behold, I send you forth as lambs among wolves"* (Luke 10:3).

If the Lamb was weak and powerless and could be defeated by wolves, why would God send us out as lambs against an enemy who is more powerful so that we would lose? Know this—God wants us to have victories and win! In the natural realm, it seems more logical to send us out as lions amongst wolves. This is not the way God sent Jesus, and this is not the way Jesus sends us. His Kingdom runs by a different system than the natural realm. In this world, it looks like the lion is stronger than the lamb, and naturally that's true, but in God's world it's not. The lamb rivals the lion's power and displays even greater strength at times. They are both needed and are equal in authority and power in God's Kingdom. Now I understand why they say in Heaven, *"Worthy is the Lamb that was slain to receive power, and riches, and wisdom, and strength, and honour, and glory, and blessing"* (Rev. 5:12). The Lion has prevailed through conquering, but the Lamb is worthy to rule (see Rev. 5:5). We can conquer but not have the ability to rule what we have conquered. This was the difference, as history records, between Philip II of Macedonia and his son Alexander the Great who conquered and ruled the whole known world.

Philip II conquered the world with brutal force and pillaging. People were forced to obey him in his conquests which made it difficult for him to rule them. People don't forget about being pillaged, tortured, mishandled, or mistreated. A very wise person in Philip II's time said that he could conquer, but he would not rule.

There are men today who are great conquerors but are poor rulers. Ruling takes a different ability than conquering. Jesus was successful at both. We need Him as the Lion to conquer, but we also need Him as the Lamb to learn to rule what we have conquered. This is what the Scripture referred to when it says that we are more than conquerors through Him that loved us (see Rom. 8:37). Someone who has moved past conquering has started to enjoy the blessing of what they've conquered. They are now governing, or ruling, what they have conquered. This is who the Lord has made us to be. This is the character of the Lamb!

Jesus Appears in Different Forms

After that He appeared in another form unto two of them as they walked (Mark 16:12).

A few years after Jesus came to me after my conversion, I thought to myself, "Why didn't He look like John described Him in the Book of Revelation with white hair, bronzed feet, and eyes of fire?" Years later, I learned that He can appear in different forms. He also said to me that the appearance in Revelation is not His only physical identity. In other words, He can appear in different forms as He did to John in Revelation. He does this to speak symbolically with a prophetic emphasis for the moment, or when He wants to relay a message. Jesus doesn't have a literal physical sword coming out of His mouth in His normal form or image as described by John in Revelation. Jesus came in a form to emphasize a specific aspect of His character. He appeared to me in His form as the Lion of Judah, but this is not His normal form.

He did this to give me a parabolic message. So don't get hung up on one form that you may hear about, such as the one John describes in the Book of Revelation. It makes sense for the Lord to change forms depending on the setting, events, or purpose. It's just like when we change clothes to go to an interview, or to a wedding; we don't put on makeup, dress in our nice suits, and wear our best shoes to go to a football game or to the grocery store. We change forms according to the event or setting.

ENDNOTES

1. "Praus": see http://www.studylight.org/lex/grk/view. cgi?number=4239.

2. Kenneth E. Hagin, *Plans, Purposes, and Pursuits* (Tulsa, OK: Faith Library Publications, Inc., 1988).

CHAPTER 6

He's Very Affectionate Toward Us

He's Jealous Over Us in His Love
Because He Loves Us

He's Very Affectionate Toward Us

HE WILL PROVOKE YOU TO JEALOUSY JUST TO SEE YOUR LOVE FOR HIM

He Wants Us to Be Jealous in Our Affections for Him
He Provoked Me to Jealousy

In the late nineties, my relationship with the Lord steadily deepened, but in a different manner. It deepened through a series of trials, temptations, and a battle with the flesh concerning complacency. I again began to slack up in my pursuit of Him, leaving behind the spiritual intensity that I had first walked in. My prayer life was waning, discouragement was trying to set in, and boredom was right in front of me. I really didn't understand why I was feeling like this. Then I began struggling in my prayer life and relationship with the Lord—there were moments that I just didn't feel like praying. After everything the Lord had done for me, I began to see that there was a danger in treating my relationship with Him lightly. But I didn't understand how I could have seen the Lord so many times already and experienced going to Heaven and still ended up feeling this way. Well, the truth is that no matter how glorious of an experience you have had with the Lord, He will allow you to go through seasons where you have to battle against the degenerative effects of the flesh and fight for your relationship with God in order to stay at the same level of intensity. This battle in our life against the flesh and the carnal man proves that we are His. *"They that are Christ's have crucified the flesh with the affections and lusts"* (Gal. 5:24). We must understand that no matter how many experiences or supernatural encounters God gives us, we are still human, and we live in this unredeemed body! When a person has appearances from Christ, it does not mean that his or her character has been perfected or that he or she has "arrived."

You must be willing to die to the flesh on a daily basis in order to keep up in your relationship with the Lord. Jesus said, *"And he that taketh not his cross, and followeth after Me, is not worthy of Me"* (see Matt. 10:38). Taking up your cross means that you are putting to death the desires of your flesh and soul. We must die daily to follow Jesus. Jesus must be pursued, but how do you keep up if you don't deny yourself and die to what your desires are? Paul said, *"I count all things but loss for the excellency of the knowledge of Christ Jesus my Lord: for whom I have suffered the loss of all things, and do count them but dung, that I may win Christ"* (see Phil. 3:8). Paul was willing to give up everything for this special relationship with the Lord and for the excellency of the knowledge of Christ!

In this visitation, the Lord came to me to provoke me to jealousy, to gently nudge and push me to the place I should have been with Him. He did this to keep me current with Him. Thank God for His mercy, because when we are experiencing moments of hindrance, He does things like this to encourage us and motivate us to get to the place we should be with Him. Well, this is what happened to me! This was so awkward to me because I never knew Jesus was like this, or would do something like this.

Oh No, She Don't!!!

This visitation took place in a matter of seconds. One night while I was asleep, the Lord came in my room, and His voice was as clear and plain as an audible voice. In this visitation, I didn't see His face, but He disclosed Himself to me by words. I heard the voice of His words so clearly during my sleep that I woke up afterward! He walked in so still, and before I knew it, He was whispering in my ear. It felt like someone was leaning over and whispering to me, when I heard a voice that said, *"There is a young lady somewhere around the world in a third-world country."* For about two seconds there was a pause—and a silence and stillness were in the atmosphere. Then with an even gentler, more peaceful, quiet whisper, He said, *"She's catching up to the same level that your relationship is at with Me!"* The whisper of His voice was so extraordinary that I woke up. I woke up with a pure and loving jealousy in my heart from this visitation, saying to myself, "Oh no, she don't!" After this I promised not to become complacent in my relationship with the Lord, nor to let anyone surpass me in my closeness and intimacy with Him. This encounter was shocking to me until I got more understanding from the Scripture about the Lord. My religious upbringing wouldn't even let me think that the Lord would say something like this.

He is passionate in His love and relationship for us, and He is not only jealous over us as the Scripture says, but He also provokes us to jealousy so that we are stimulated and motivated to passionately and intimately pursue Him. From this encounter, I also realized that the Lord had given me a unique relationship that seemed not only to be beyond most Americans' relationships, but that even rivaled those in third-world countries. This was amazing to me because, again, I didn't know what level I was on in my relationship with Him, plus I didn't know what great thing I had done to get to this place with Him. All I thought was, "I just love Him." I thought this was normal for a Christian, so I didn't see my efforts to get close to God as something extraordinary. This visitation served both as a slight correction, and as a profound and encouraging truth—the Lord saw my relationship with Him as parallel to none! Don't you want this relationship with Him? You can have it! But you have to outrun me to get it! I'm laughing while writing this part of the book. Isn't the Lord so wonderful?

HE'S JEALOUS OVER US

*Thus saith the Lord of hosts; **I am jealous for Jerusalem and for Zion with a great jealousy*** (Zechariah 1:14).

Our God is a jealous God, and He has been known to use jealousy to provoke His people when they were getting complacent or distracted in their relationship with Him. This has been recorded throughout history in the Scriptures. The Lord Himself said it; listen to Him in this Scripture:

*Thou shalt not bow down thyself to them, nor serve them: for **I the Lord thy God am a jealous God*** (Exodus 20:5).

It is also very obvious in Scripture that the Lord wants us to be jealous over Him with a godly jealousy. The Lord even says in the New Testament,

I will provoke you to jealousy (Romans 10:19).

You see, there is a pure, godly jealousy in the Holy Spirit realm that is unlike the impure jealousy in our flesh that leads to anger, cruelty, and can even result in homicide. This is called the spirit of jealousy, and satan uses this spirit to murder and treat others cruelly. That is the jealousy of the world, but godly jealousy that is used by Him is holy and pure. The first time that the word *jealous* appears in the Old Testament, it is translated from the Hebrew word qana, which means, *"to be zealous or to make zealous over another or for another."*[1] The word for jealousy in the New

Testament is the same word for *zealous*. The New Testament word for *zealous* in the Greek *zelos,* which has a little more depth of meaning: *"to have warmth of feelings for or against, to also have desire to become boiling, or have ferventness."*[2]

HE WANTS US TO HAVE A GODLY JEALOUSY OVER HIM.

Jesus. He is jealous over His relationship with us, and He wants us to be jealous over our relationship with Him in a godly way!

Intimacy Driven

My Life's Pursuit—"To Be Close To Him"

He reminded me of my initial conversion through a face-to-face encounter I had with Him in 1989, and I remembered how much I loved Him. Honestly, my main prayer every day for two to three years after my conversion was that I wanted to sit at His feet for all eternity, just to be close to Him and next to Him always. My prayer was this, "Lord, I know You promised in the new life to build us mansions, but all I really want is that You will give me a place at Your feet to wash them, so that I never have to be away from You."

I just wanted to be close to Him, not because I wanted a position next to Him, but because I loved Him, and wanted to have a close relationship with Him. This was my strong desire, prayer, and request of the Lord for three years after I got saved. For a while, I thought it was a corny or weird prayer. I didn't know if the Lord would even answer a prayer like that. The cry of my heart was for an extraordinary closeness, and I didn't know how to put this into words. So I expressed it through asking if I could be close in this way—by asking that I wash His feet with my tears so that I never had to leave His side for all of eternity. I loved Him that much because I realize how He first loved me. All I could think about was how He gave His total life for me on the cross. As a result of this, I was willing to give Him my total life back as a response to His love for me. After seeing Jesus for the first time, and having out-of-body experiences that took me to the third heaven, I loved Him so much that I was ready to die and go to Heaven. I didn't want to stay here anymore. I got bored easily, depressed, and very discouraged.

I had to learn to deal with the discouragement and depression of coming from a place so glorious. But most of all, I had to deal with depression in this realm because I was away from the One I loved, Jesus, who has the greatest personality in the world. I'm not exaggerating. He has the greatest personality in the world! His personality is so wonderful to be around. I'm sure you would have felt the same way, too. Later I learned that it was selfish of me to want to go to my heavenly home early, because the Lord had explained to me that He had a work for me to do that would benefit His children and His Kingdom. I didn't know that this intense love and desire would one day lead to all of this. Jesus gave one condition in our relationship with Him for Him to manifest and appear. John described it his Gospel, *"He that loveth Me"* (John 14:21). It's all about loving Him. As I said earlier, this is a love covenant relationship! Another element that I believed the Lord used in my life was the void that I had always felt from the time I was a little child.

"The Key": Being Open Hearted to Intimacy

To explain this, I must tell you this little story of my childhood that the Lord reminded me of. This story opened my eyes to see the passion and potential I had for relationship. Before I tell you what this was, I must say I am taking a great risk to show you my heart. I could be criticized or accused of homosexuality for what I am about to tell you. This is not a story about playing with dolls, nor does it have to do with anything related to homosexuality. I did not play with Barbie dolls as a little boy. I was like other little boys, and I am a staunch believer that little boys should play with toys for boys, and little girls should play with toys for girls. Most boys are drawn to male role model toys, and most girls are drawn to female role model toys. That's not to say that boys and girls don't play with other kinds of toys, but when I was growing up boys played with their G.I. Joes and action figures, and girls played with Barbies and baby dolls.

When I was a small child of about seven or eight years old, I had this overwhelming passion and love to one day meet a woman who would be my wife, and whom I would love in a very deep and special way. I remember when my grandfather lived with us (my mother's father) we would share the same room. As a little boy this passion was so strong, that I would go and sneak my little sister's beautiful Barbie doll, and at night I would lay it in the bed next to me so that I could envision this woman. I would think romantically of the deep love relationship and emotional intimacy that I would have with my future wife. As I grew into a teenager, I thought that this intense desire was not real, and that maybe I was a little overboard in having these emotions and desire to love and be loved in this way. I'll never forget a very hilarious morning after I had snuck one of my little sister's Barbie dolls into bed with me. In the morning, my bigger brother Richard caught me with the doll in bed. He yelled and hollered, "Mama, David got that Barbie doll in the bed again!" I laugh now at this, but back then it wasn't so humorous. When my brother caught me with the doll, he would tell my mother on me. As a little boy, I didn't know what was going on with me.

I didn't understand my very deep passion and desire to have a very special love relationship with a woman, one in which she would love me in the same deep way that I loved her. As a young boy, I realized that I wanted to have a mature relationship with the love of my life; it wasn't just a surface thing. I also wondered years later, "Is this the way a man should feel about a woman?" You see, in our culture it is usually the women who show more passion and love in a deeply intimate and romantic way. Men don't seem to display their emotions and passions beyond surface level expression. Where I'm from, men were taught that they are supposed to control their emotions. Even ministers were taught this to the degree that they couldn't express their emotions freely to the Lord in worship.

Pride Hinders Our Intimacy

I found out from the Lord that this was a grave mistake in Western and American culture. It's wrong for men to think that women should be the only ones to display their intense love for their husbands, and that men should return their affection with

185

little emotional intimacy. This is backwards. Men were created with the capacity to love women in a greater way than women could love men, because men were commanded to love their wives just as Christ loves His Church (see Eph. 5:25). We were created first, and were commanded to love intimately first! We have even caused women to have this mentality that they are attracted to men who are harsh and rough, showing hardly any emotion at all. Women have expected this to be normal for men. This is not normal at all, and it is a direct result of man's fallen nature, and the pride that has entered it!

Pride is what causes men to do this. Now I'm not talking about men being effeminate or girly. A man should be a man, but I'm talking about a man having the capacity to love in a deep intimate way without reservations, while being secure in his manhood at the same time. Jesus had to teach me later in life that there was nothing wrong with a man loving a woman this way. He said to me, *"David, that's the way I created man to love in the beginning."* Then He continued, *"That's how I love...deeply, intimately, and with great feeling. Men were created to love their spouse this way, as I love the Church, but pride and hardness of heart have taken the place of a tender and meek heart, David, as a result of the Fall of man and sin."* He then said to me, *"That's what I came back to restore."* Jesus wants to restore the broken fellowship between God and man, between man and man, and between man and woman. He continued, *"It's really the man's job to love the woman like you have felt is normal for a woman to love a man. The order is backwards now. Turn it back around again, David."*

I thought that this desire to be loved on such a deep and intimate level was just a Barbie doll fantasy, but I found out later that it was real. I wanted a relationship in which we could look deeply into each other's eyes, and it would be the equivalent of doing something big and special for each other. In my dreams, it was the small and simple things that meant so much. Our emotions and love for each other was so intense that the simple act of looking at each other would cause butterflies to gently flap inside my heart.

Intimacy
"The Emotional Expression of Love"

I cannot express in words how wonderful this feeling of love was. All I know is that this would cause me to cry hot tears that would stream down my face and into my pillow when I was seven years old. These were not tears of sadness, but tears full of an intense love that I wanted to experience with a woman who would one day be my wife. Little did I know that God would use that passion as a catalyst for my relationship with Him and Jesus! These were not boo-hoo tears. Instead, they were silent tears that were very intense emotionally. I could feel the warmth of these tears streaming down my face. They were not cold tears; the romantic feeling I felt inside my heart like butterflies was so very tender and passionate. When I'm experiencing Jesus' presence today, whether in a service or in prayer by myself, I feel this same way, but the ecstasy is a thousand times more intense. When I get on stage during a service to start worshiping, people have wondered why I start weeping or sobbing profusely. Well, this is the reason, and this is what I experience! It's like butterflies; I feel like I've been raptured into Heaven by His love every time! This is what I'm feeling when tears are streaming down my eyes in prayer alone, in a service during a crusade, or just when I'm sitting in someone else's service where the presence of God visits. In almost every service (without exaggeration), I feel like I'm being caught up into Heaven with

Him all over again. I have felt this way in every service ever since I got saved in 1989 at the age of 17. The tears are so warm and hot, and they just keep coming from the intensity of experiencing His presence when He comes in a room. I really love Jesus.

Today I'm at a point where honestly I feel like I have nothing—nothing to give Him but my love, and I love Him with all my heart. He's all I have. He's really all I've got! I've given up everything and have suffered the loss of everything just to have Him! The intensity and the ecstasy of His presence is amazing, life-changing, and has become all I look forward too. I'm addicted to His presence and person! I have just got to have Him. There was a time when I loved Him because I needed Him. I can honestly say today that this has changed—I now need Him because I love Him!

The Love Covenant With Jesus
"Beyond the Love for a Woman"

And they two made a covenant before the Lord (1 Samuel 23:18).

*I am distressed for thee, my brother Jonathan: very pleasant hast thou been unto me: **thy love to me was wonderful, passing the love of women*** (2 Samuel 1:26).

David and Jonathan's covenant relationship was a shadow and type of the love relationship we can have with Christ. David was a type of Christ, and Jonathan symbolizes us. The Bible says that this brotherly love surpassed the love of women, but it's referring to the love we can have with God that fulfills us beyond the love we have for our spouses or the opposite sex. The word *love* in this context comes from the root Hebrew word *ahab* which means, *"To have af-*

fection or like for a friend."[3] David mentioned how wonderful Jonathan's friendship love was to him. The word *wonderful* in this context comes from the Hebrew word *pala* which means, *"remarkable, a miracle, a marvelous thing."*[4] This denotes that this love relationship is a supernatural and miraculous love. It is marvelous like David said. It is totally remarkable! Do you want to experience a miraculous and supernatural love relationship with the Lord? I'm a witness that it is remarkable, miraculous, and supernatural love that surpasses the natural love we have for the opposite sex. This love, in fact, is a secret. It's the same type of love that Jesus describes when He told us to go in our secret closet to pray and be alone with the Lord in fellowship. He promised that the Father would reward us openly by this secret relationship. The reward is having Him personally manifested openly. Today, in a world where homosexuality is so widespread and accepted as normal, I must make a distinction here that the love that David and Jonathan had for each other was not impure. They were not homosexuals. It was a supernatural and pure love in the form of a godly covenant between them. The Bible mentions this:

> *Therefore thou shalt deal kindly with thy servant; for thou hast brought thy servant into a covenant of the Lord with thee...So Jonathan made a covenant with the house of David, saying, Let the Lord even require it at the hand of David's enemies. And Jonathan caused David to swear again, because he loved him: for he loved him as he loved his own soul"* (1 Samuel 20:8,16-17).

Jonathan loved David not only beyond the love he had for the opposite sex, but also beyond the love for his father and his own life, as Christ commanded us to love Him. He said, *"If any man come to Me, and not hate his father, and mother, and wife* [passing the love of women], *and children, and brethren, and sisters, yea, and his own life also* [his own soul], *he cannot be My disciple"* (Luke 14:26; see Matt. 10:37-38). This kind of love passes the love I always wanted with a woman. I thought what I was feeling for a woman was romantic and ecstatic! But when I moved into this covenant realm of relationship and fellowship with Jesus, I personally was completely overcome and overwhelmed with His love for me! It changed my life. Although those natural feelings are still there that God put in me to have for a woman, this love for Jesus has superseded anything that I have ever experienced or felt. It was an intimacy beyond ecstasy. Now I understand better through experience, in a more mature sense, what the Holy Spirit spoke through Paul when He said, *"and to know the love of Christ, which passeth knowledge"* (Eph. 3:19).

His Love Surpasses the Knowledge and Understanding of All Things

This love relationship with Him passes the knowledge of anything you can understand at this present time or for all eternity. It passes the deepest love you know, or have ever experienced with the opposite sex. This is what this love covenant is about when Jesus mentions it to us in John 14:21, *"He that hath My commandments, and keepeth them, he it is that loveth Me: and he that loveth Me shall be loved of My Father, and I will love him."* In other words, He will allow us to experience and feel this relationship with Him. The Bible says that the Lord first loved us and that this love is what prompted our love toward Him, not that we earn His love through keeping His commandments (see 1 John 4:10). The love spoken by Jesus in John 14:21 means something else. In other words, He's saying that He will manifest the love He has for us to us and before others. This is the same love He has for everyone else (because God is no respecter of persons). He loves everyone equally, but He doesn't boldly, openly display this love as He does for those who are in covenant with Him. But He does manifest this love for us by allowing us to see Him face-to-face, while displaying to others how much He loves us. Men have entered into covenants through the ages. But David and Jonathan's covenant was made before the Lord. This means God was in the mix of this love covenant that Jonathan and David made between themselves. The Bible says that *God is love; and he that dwelleth in love dwelleth in God"* (1 John 4:16). This confirms that this was not a covenant made between just two men. The Lord left this on record so that we could know it is possible to walk in a deep, intimate covenant of love with Him. This covenant surpasses the knowledge that we have of our intimacy with the opposite sex.

This love goes beyond and surpasses all knowledge about anything anywhere, for all time and for all eternity! It is supernatural. The neat thing about all this is that you can have this too! You can experience this intimacy beyond ecstasy that Jesus longs to show you through having a face-to-face relationship with Him. You can have a relationship in which He continually appears to you in the physical realm and in other ways that He chooses to come to you! I can't decide or tell you in which fashion or manner He will come and appear to you, but I do know that He will come. That's simply it; He promises to come!

He's A Person Who Loves His Enemies Deeply...Even Judas

His Passionate Eyes and Heart

I say unto you, love your enemies (Matthew 5:44).

As I kept learning by watching Jesus' actions, one of the main lessons He taught me is how thoroughly and deeply He loves, not only His people but His enemies. In this next appearance I had from the Lord, He came to me again during my sleep to awake and show me a great truth of how He genuinely loves His enemies, even those who betray Him. Jesus said in Matthew 5:44, *"But I say unto you, love your enemies."* When He came and got me in my sleep, He took my spirit out of my body. Jesus spoke to me, saying, *"I want to show you a great truth about the time right before I died, and how I even loved Judas..."*

We all know what a horrible and unthinkable thing Judas did to Jesus. I know what he did was very dark, but Jesus still loved him deeply. Even though Judas lost his soul to satan as a consequence of his actions, Jesus didn't say, "Well you betrayed Me. Just go to hell like you're supposed to." No, He had compassion for him.

Taken to See Jerusalem in Jesus' Time

As I stood there, Jesus immediately beamed me (I don't know how, it just happened) to the past and showed me the location where Judas committed suicide in Jerusalem. He allowed me to watch the events of what happened that very day over 2000 years ago.

I don't know how, but what I do know is that I was standing there watching the events unfold after Jesus' death on the cross; Jesus allowed me to watch. We were in Jerusalem, Israel. As I stood suspended in midair watching, I saw this old-looking tree that grew out of a rocky cliff edge. It looked like one of those old trees that grows in the Middle East out of the stone and has branches that hang over the cliff. This cliff had a deep and long bottom to it. It was a stony area.

As I watched, I saw Judas (after he had just betrayed Jesus hours earlier), climb up this tree with a rope to hang himself. I saw how he chose a branch that was hanging over the edge of a deep cliff. He was kneeling on his knees on a tree branch and threw a rope to the end of the branch where it hung over the cliff. I observed as he put the rope around his neck and tied it to the tree branch to hang himself. Then he jumped down out of the tree, his body hanging as he died. His body was droopy as he dangled high over the deep drop beneath him.

Then Jesus showed me a great truth. Immediately following Jesus' death at the cross, He commended His spirit into the Father's hand:

And when Jesus had cried with a loud voice, He said, Father, into thy hands I commend My Spirit: and having said thus, He gave up the ghost (Luke 23:46).

I saw the actual scene when the Father had separated the spirit of Jesus from His body on the cross. As Jesus allowed me to observe what was going on, I glimpsed at how His mind was on the next thing His Father wanted Him to do, which was go to hell to preach to the lost spirits, but before He did this, I saw Jesus make a stop by Judas' grave site, the tree on which he had hanged himself. According to Matthew 27:1-7, Judas betrayed Jesus in the morning and then went and hanged himself. Jesus, however, didn't give up the ghost until later that evening. So according to Scripture, Judas was already dead on the tree. I researched these details later when I woke up from this visitation.

Jesus Showed Me His Compassion for Judas

As Jesus came to the tree where Judas was dangling, I knew He was on a mission and assignment from the Father to go to hell and take the keys of hell and death, and to bring up the old saints like David, Jeremiah, and others. Before He did, He was permitted by the Father to stop and look at Judas. Jesus had a white robe on His spiritual body. At this point, He was in His spirit form because His body was dead on the cross. Jesus showed me the actual events that took place in the spirit realm right after His death on the cross. He didn't stay at Judas' suicide location long, but in His compassion, He did stop by. As Jesus allowed me to gaze at Him, I saw how He walked up to Judas, who was now dead and drooping there, and said with great sadness, hurt, compassion, and great love, the words, *"Oh, Judas."*

The expression on His face for Judas was so astonishing to me. I saw this Man, Jesus, the Son of God, who was betrayed by the one who ate bread with Him, show a love and compassion that is beyond this world for Judas who turned out to be His enemy. Many people don't understand how Jesus really loved Judas, although Judas had become his enemy, and he did not make it to Heaven. Then Jesus' actions became clear to me, and I thought of the Scripture that records Judas coming into the garden with soldiers to betray Him. The Bible states that Jesus didn't scold or rebuke him but called him *friend*.

> *And Jesus said unto him, Friend, wherefore art thou come?* (Matthew 26:50).

Jesus displayed love to Judas all the way until after His death. Jesus never changed toward him; He loved Judas until the end. If you study, you will see that Jesus knew from the beginning that Judas was going to betray Him, but He walked in love toward him and did not expose Judas to the other apostles. Have you ever noticed how the other apostles never knew the one who would betray Jesus? Even when they asked, He still answered them in a way that prevented them from figuring out that Judas was the one. For the Scripture records that after satan entered his heart, Judas immediately left the table, but the disciples thought Judas had an errand to do concerning money.

He's a Person of Love

His Love Covers

Judas' betrayal was not known to the others until he betrayed Jesus with a kiss, exposing himself. Jesus allowed His enemy to be with Him all that time, without revealing and uncovering him in front of the others. Wow! What love! This is the same love that is described in the Bible when it says, *"Love covers over the multitude of sins"* (1 Pet. 4:8 NIV). What integrity Jesus had, that even until the "kiss of betrayal," Jesus called Judas *friend*. Jesus was faithful to Judas. This convicted me, because I realized that I had not been this way to my enemies and those I felt had betrayed me in some way. I saw how Jesus didn't struggle to love His enemies; He loved completely, thoroughly. This was amazing to me. Another point that I would like to make here regards something I always had a question about because the Bible didn't give every detail of Judas' death. In Matthew 27:5, Judas hanged himself. But in Acts 1:18, Judas fell headlong, burst asunder in the midst, and all his bowels gushed out.

And he cast down the pieces of silver in the temple, and departed, and went and hanged himself (Matthew 27:5).

Now this man purchased a field with the reward of iniquity; and falling headlong, he burst asunder in the midst, and all his bowels gushed out (Acts 1:18).

I have read these passages for years, and they sounded inconsistent to me. In one passage it sounded like Judas committed suicide by jumping and falling off the cliff, but in another passage the Bible says Judas fell headlong. Through this visitation, I saw how he could hang himself and fall headlong with his bowels gushing out. It said he *fell* headlong, not jumped. When we usually think of someone hanging themselves on a rope, we usually picture a floor not far underneath them. I was picturing his death from this point of view. How could he hang not too far from the ground and then fall headlong with his bowels gushing out? After Jesus took me to the location in Jerusalem in this face-to-face encounter, I saw the events as they transpired; the Lord explained this to me. Judas, after tying himself to the edge of a branch, dangled over a steep stone wall that had a long drop with stones at the bottom. You see, after Jesus left the cross in His spirit form, He stopped by Judas hanging on the limb that evening. Judas had been hanging all day, since that morning until the Lord passed by to see him and bereave his death.

I saw the branch break from the weight of Judas' body after some time. The branch was not a very thick branch, but it was strong enough to hold his body up for a while until the weight of his body bent the branch, and it suddenly snapped. The initial impact of his body hitting the ground caused his body to burst and his bowels to gush out just like the Scriptures said. Before his body made impact with the ground, it turned in midair with his head facing down toward the ground. The collision of his body against the stone ground burst his body, and his bowels gushed out. This can only happen when someone has fallen a long distance!

Jesus looked at Judas with great compassion and with an expression of love, deep hurt, and sorrow on His face. He then turned, walking with diligence to the next thing on His mind, which was His assignment from the Father. I knew in this visitation He was going to preach in hell. Then Jesus said to me, *"David, I brought you here to show you the events that took place with Judas' death, but most of all to show you the great compassion and love I have for My friends, even when they betray. I loved Judas very much, David."* He went on to say, *"I also want to show you how you are to love your enemies, even those who are among My people, like Judas was. I showed you these events that you might learn to love like I love, not just unto death, but beyond your death."* Then He said to me, *"David, love your enemies like I love My enemies. I love you; now you love them."* Then He concluded, saying, *"This command I now give you—love them."*

Loving Our Enemies

HE TAUGHT ME HOW TO LOVE MY ENEMIES.

It's amazing to see how deep Jesus' love goes. He said, *"All that the Father giveth Me shall come to Me; and him that cometh to Me I will in no wise cast out"* (John 6:37). He didn't cast Judas out. He cast demons out, but not people. The Lord allowed people to walk away and stop following Him, like the seventy, but He never cast them out.

> *From that time many of His disciples went back, and walked no more with Him* (John 6:66).

This was love. I saw how I didn't love my enemies like Jesus did. I mistreated my Judases. I saw how I put people out of the ministry, and was so easily ready to dismiss them when they betrayed me. I saw how I didn't love my enemies like I was supposed to. Jesus then taught me how He never put one person out of His ministry. He said that *"Him that cometh to me, **I will in no wise cast him out!**"* (John 6:37). He also stated that this was the will of His Father—everyone the Father had entrusted to Him would come to Him. Jesus would for no reason cast His followers out, or lose them in any way, but instead redeemed and raised them up again (see John 6:37,39,44).

> *And this is the Father's will which hath sent Me, that of all which He hath given Me I should lose nothing* (John 6:39).

This is Jesus' character. He promises never to reject us or put us out. I wasn't like this. I thought putting people out when they rebelled was the best thing. I've found a better way! After learning this, I became so heartbroken and full of godly sorrow over the people that I had treated this way. I also thought this was the right thing because I had seen so many other leaders do the same thing, but as I matured, I saw that this did not match Jesus' character. I am so sorry for this mistake I made, and I want to say to those who may have experienced this from my early ministry that I am so deeply sorry, and I love you.

For three and a half years Jesus never revealed to the apostles His betrayer even when He knew who he was when he first chose his disciples. What great love! I was appalled at myself when I looked back and saw how I had been the total opposite from the character of Christ. I didn't love my enemies, because love covers even the faults and sins of your enemies. Did I cover the sins of my enemies? Had I done this? The answer was No! I thought I loved my enemies until this shocking appearance from the Lord showed me how Jesus had loved Judas even though Judas had betrayed Him.

What I've Seen of Jesus

Every time Jesus gracefully granted me the opportunity to see Him again, a new dimension of His personality was revealed to me. As He has stood in front of me face-to-face, I have seen that Jesus is very personable. He is a person, and He has a personality. From the things that I've seen, I would say that Jesus is a very cordial person. He is a man of very few words, but when He speaks, every sentence from His lips is filled with such great substance, revelation, and deep understanding beyond what your mind can humanly perceive at the moment that He's talking to you. He's very mild tempered and has a soft, approachable, and easygoing personality. He is like this for the most part, except under certain circumstances.

He is a gentle man (gentleman). This means that He exercises balance and sensitivity toward others by not being a burden by putting too much pressure or stress on individuals. He is sensitive to know and consider how much each individual person can handle. This comes from His meek personality which exercises gentleness as a result of what He knows about each person. He is the most loving man that you would ever want to meet, and His eyes are full of compassion for us. He is austere, firm, and serious when He needs to be. He does not accept illegitimate excuses, but at the same time He exercises great compassion, pity, and mercy. He is humble and never assumes or presumes a position or place of authority without being asked to do so.

Instead, He chooses to walk in the low place, never striving ambitiously for the high position. These are the mannerisms that I've seen while literally being face-to-face with Jesus. When encountering His presence and personality, the atmosphere is filled with peace, serenity, love, and light. In His presence, there is such freedom from strife, war, and condemnation for your sins and mistakes. There is freedom from feeling rejected and unacceptable as a result of not living up to His standards. There's no condemnation while standing in His presence. He never condemns. He loves, encourages, and forgives. There is no fear of being rejected, but instead an invitation to approach and come to Him.

He has a personality which invites others to come to Him and follow Him. He is so hospitable.

When you stand in front of Him, His eyes search inside of you, into your heart. His eyes are like flickering flames of fire that see right through you and lay everything out about your personality. There is a sense of total transparency while in His presence; there is nothing hidden from Him. He is a man of intense intimacy, and He loves fellowship with you more than you can ever realize. He is definitely a morning person and loves His fellowship at this time of the day with you. His ability to have friendships that are intimate is off the chart! Will you hurt Him by rejecting His invitation to you for this intimacy? He calls you to this intimacy. He is a very real person who can be hurt, you know, especially when we neglect our moments of communion with Him. I saw this on His face.

He is a powerful King and Emperor and a man of great authority. He walks in authority and government, but with a mild mannered, soft, gentle, and lowly attitude about Him. He is a man of intense love, and He has a very friendly nature. His words are tender, soft, and peaceful. I understand now why Elijah wrapped his face in cloth when he heard God's voice. The Lord's voice has such tremendous and amazing characteristics to it, and when heard, it affects your whole being. His voice is like a texture and sound that you have never heard. He has a very quiet side to His personality and doesn't volunteer information when not asked. There is no one like Him in Heaven or on earth! He is a joy to be around, and I have so enjoyed all the time we've spent face-to-face. Now I was about to see firsthand and face-to-face that He is a morning person and how much this time of the day means to Him!

ENDNOTES

1. "Qana": see http://www.studylight.org/lex/heb/view.cgi?number=07065.

2. "Zelos": see http://www.studylight.org/lex/grk/view.cgi?number=2205.

3. "Ahab": see http://www.studylight.org/lex/heb/view.cgi?number=0157.

4. "Pala": see http://www.studylight.org/lex/heb/view.cgi?number=06381.

He Is a Morning Person

The Mornings: His Daily
Appointments With You

CHAPTER 7

He Is a Morning Person

JESUS VALUES THE TIME YOU SPEND WITH HIM IN THE MORNINGS.

During the fall of 1997, I had just finished a long season of seeking the Lord that started in the summer of 1996 and carried through until the spring of 1997. I was going back and forth to the church to do all week shut-ins where I would fast, pray, consecrate myself, intercede, and repent—letting the Lord deal with me on some personal issues. One night when I fell fast asleep, there Jesus was again in my dream. He had on the usual beautiful white robe that He mostly wears when I see Him. In this face-to-face experience with Him, He was sitting instead of standing. Jesus was sitting on a white rock with His head in His hand and looking in the opposite direction of where I was at. He did not look like He normally looked, but had an expression on His face of disappointment, sadness, and hurt.

This time He looked different; He looked sad. As I walked up to Him, I said, "Lord, I miss You." I knew something was wrong because I had never seen Him look in the opposite direction when we would meet face-to-face. Before this encounter, He had always turned to look me directly in my eyes, face-to-face, when He would talk to me. I learned that it's an honor for someone to look you in the face and talk to you directly face-to-face. When a person does not look you in the face, it is a sign of disapproval or disappointment. His countenance tells it all.

I had slacked up in spending time with the Lord in the mornings at this point. After my conversion, I used to spend time praying three times a day—morning, noon, and evening. Although I was spending vast amounts of time in the noon hour and during the evening, I didn't understand how important our morning times were to Him. As Christians, I'm sure you know what I mean—the complacency, boredom, tests, and trials that we all struggle with from time to time. Years later, I found out why the mornings mean so much to Him during our communion time, and I have included it in this book. It's mandatory that you know how important your morning times with Him are too! The reason that I told Him I missed Him was that I felt emptiness inside of me. Whenever you have an intense relationship with the Lord where you spend hours together you can start to feel empty if you slack up even for a short time like two weeks.

HE MISSED HIS TIME WITH ME

When I walked up to Jesus, He never turned to look me in my face which was very unusual. His behavior was hurtful to me, but I knew there had to be a legitimate reason. After I said, "Lord, I miss You," He then replied in such a loving, soft, peaceful tone, but with deep hurt in His voice, "*I miss you too, and the times we used to spend in the mornings.*" When He expressed these feelings, I saw the heart of Jesus. My heart dropped, and immediately I woke up in tears saying, "Lord, I'm sorry. I will spend time with You in the mornings again!" At this I rushed out of the bed and ran into the bathroom to be with Him in prayer. It was about 3:00 A.M. This visitation seemed like it only lasted for about ten seconds before I woke up. I didn't realize how selfish I had been in neglecting my relationship and prayer time with Him. I had hurt Him, and I didn't realize what I had done until years later. This was amazing because I got a chance to see His heart and how He feels. I felt honored. Who was I for Him to show me His heart like this? He actually missed His time with little old me? I was not sensitive to His feelings and didn't realize He would miss me like this. Who was I? It never occurred to me that being with me like this would mean so much to the most powerful man in the universe, the King of kings, and a potentate. There were billions more people in the world; who was I? I thought it was the normal duty of prayer. But it was more to Him than this. It was serious! This was one of the most hurtful times of my walk with the Lord that I can remember, but also one of the most satisfying times to realize how much our relationship meant to Him.

He was trying to teach me the importance of the morning times with Him, but I didn't understand it then. I thought afterward, "Why would He mention only our communion time in the mornings in a specific manner like this? Why weren't all the other times of the day that I was still praying during the noon hour and evening not mentioned by Him? Why did He specifically mention our morning times like this?" At the time, it didn't dawn on me that this was a glorious revelation about morning time prayer with Him. Years later, I would come to understand why Jesus responded this way about our morning times. I would also come to find out more than He explained to me at the time, a deep revelation about what the mornings mean to Him.

You see, I was behind in my study of His Word. There are things that we are supposed to know from spending time with the Lord in the study of His Word. I spent many hours in prayer and fellowship with the Lord, and with the Holy Spirit, but I didn't study the Bible thoroughly enough about subjects like I should have. It wasn't Jesus' job to tell me in face-to-face encounters (which I didn't understand at that time). I would have never made these unthinkable mistakes if I had known that it was my job to search, seek, and find out these truths. I learned three major points from this experience with Jesus.

He Misses His Time With You

The main thing I recognized from seeing the expression of love and deep hurt on Jesus' face is that He didn't want any ounce of our time lost in the mornings. I saw how much He desires our fellowship, more than we can ever desire His. You see, He has a deeper capacity to love us and spend time with us than we do with Him. When we don't commune with Him, He misses His time with us. If you have slacked up in your prayer with the Lord, He misses His time with you! He's saying to you now, *"I miss My time with you!"* I saw from Jesus' facial expression how much our prayer times and fellowship mean to Him. I saw how serious it was to Him not to miss this fellowship in prayer, especially during the mornings. I thought after this visitation, "All those times before this visit, He was really right there with me when I would pray in the morning, even though I did not see Him." After I saw Him, I thought about how real those prayer times were with Him when I would feel His presence. I didn't really realize how real He was in that prayer room with me during our morning times. This all happened just because I didn't see Him in there with me all those times, even though I felt His presence. How lightly we take our prayer times just because we don't physically see Jesus in there with us! This appearance from Him and what He said actually helped me to realize that even though I didn't see Him physically with my eyes in my prayer times, He was personally always there. I recognized this when He said to me, *"And the times we used to spend in the mornings."*

HE'S REALLY THERE WITH YOU.

Believing It Consciously

Well, I was never that aware or conscious that He was that close. That's the point I'm trying to make—we are never aware unless we make a conscious effort to be aware. Jacob said, *"Surely the Lord is in this place; and I knew it not"* (Gen. 28:16). When you become God conscious, you lose sight of yourself. You begin to *"wist not"* as Moses did after he was in the Lord's presence for forty days (see Exod. 34:29). It takes time for our brain to catch up with the Lord's glory that is moving at light-speed. How many times have you been in your regular prayer time and ignored the fact that the Lord was personally there? We must start consciously—not religiously—believing that He's there. Now if you saw Him walk in and sit down by you during your prayer time, you would acknowledge His presence immediately, knowing that He is right there with you and not in a distant place. If this happened, your prayer and words would change! All I'm saying is we get into this religious mode of prayer and forget to consciously remember that the Lord is actually physically in our room even though we cannot see Him.

I thought about all the times I had prayed in the morning and how dull my mind was before He sharpened it with this statement which let me know He is with me in a real and personal way. After that experience, I started believing that He was literally with me (even though I didn't see Him) during every moment of my prayer time with Him. This experience showed me He was really there with me. My prayer life took a drastic turn from there. You must believe He's really there in that place with you when you pray! You see, I believed that He was always there with me mentally, but my mind and heart didn't always make a conscious decision to be aware of it, nor that He was there at those very moments I prayed!

There's a difference between just believing something in the mental realm and actually walking consciously in faith toward a thing or person. Like so many others, I was praying, but was unaware of how close He was to me. So when I knew this, my faith level changed when I went to meet Him in prayer. He said, *"I will not leave you comfortless: I will come to you"* (John 14:18). The Holy Spirit is always with us here on earth. Right before this Scripture, Jesus mentions that He would send us another Comforter, which was the Holy Spirit. In this verse, Jesus also mentions that He Himself would come personally to us! Not only would the Holy Spirit comfort us, but He, too, wouldn't leave us comfortless.

Jesus promises to join the Holy Spirit on earth by also coming to comfort us. Jesus promises here that He would come to us, my friends. Oh, how wonderful. You can expect a face-to-face visit from the Lord just through this promise alone! That's what He does when we pray and commune with Him—only we are not aware or conscious at the time of how close He really is during our prayer. Jesus actually comes to us in prayer. We must pay close attention to Him and be consciously and mentally aware of this.

Check His Countenance

His Countenance Tells It All

The second thing that I've learned in this appearance with Jesus is that when He appears, His countenance tells it all. His facial expression shows if He's hurt, wounded, disappointed, or displeased. He wears His emotions on His face. So you must learn to check His countenance. Believe me when I tell you this—His

211

face says it all. The point is that if you do not see His face, how can you tell? It's important for us to check His countenance and to pursue His approval.

From this visitation, I also learned that Jesus' facial expression and countenance can prophesy the condition of your relationship with Him. For instance, I had one young man ask me, "Why doesn't He show me His face?" I replied, "Usually when you don't see the Lord's face in a visitation appearance, you may see a bright light with maybe His clothes and a voice speaking out of this light. This means there's a formal quality or a lack of intimacy somewhere in your relationship with the Lord." Being face-to-face and seeing Him plainly is the highest level of intimacy that there is. I noticed this from this visitation concerning Jesus and me.

His face was turned in the opposite direction of me, even when He began speaking to me. He never turned His head or face to look me in the eye as He would normally do. This spoke of a problem in our intimacy. A lack of seeing His face also represents a lack of intimacy, and it does show you your current intimacy level with the Lord. There is a vast revelation about how the countenance of the Lord and His face affects us. Since we are talking about having a face-to-face relationship with the Lord, I thought this revelation about His countenance and facial expressions would be very important! Israel and the biblical Jewish culture knew this revelation of what it meant to seek the Lord's face.

It not only means to pray and inquire of Him, but it also means to check His countenance. It means to check out His facial expressions on any subject or even about whether or not you're in right standing with Him. It's similar to when your dad or mom would give you a wink with their eye—they didn't have to say a thing to you, but you knew by their facial expression that they were pleased with you, and that meant it was OK. During this visitation in 1997, I was about 25 years old, and I didn't understand the importance of these details that I saw in Jesus' face like I do today.

How Did I Miss This?

If I had this knowledge back then, I would have never responded the way I did. That is, even though I felt hurt and convicted about what Jesus told me, I still didn't have the total understanding and revelation of what He deeply meant. If I would have had this understanding about His countenance or the revelation of spending my mornings with Him I could have responded better after He had appeared to me. A person's face tells it all.

That's why we should look at Jesus' countenance by seeking His face. We have used and handled the Word of God so lightly and have taken it for granted. We really don't believe or take literally what the Lord is saying when He said, *"Seek ye My Face"* (Ps. 27:8; see 1 Chron. 16:11). Ask yourself, "Why would He tell us to seek His face if it meant that we couldn't find it?" We have allowed the one Scripture that says, *"No man can see My face and live,"* to set the course of our whole theology about seeing the face of God; we've completely thrown out or overlooked others like, *"Seek My Face!"* (Exod. 33:20; see 1 Chron. 16:11).

We don't take this literally like we should, but God means just what He says. Jesus said, *"Seek, and ye shall find"* (Matt. 7:7). If you seek the face of the Lord, you will find it! This call from God to seek His face is the great calling we fell from during the Fall of Adam. Remember, Adam could see the Lord before He sinned! The call from God to seek His face is also a call to reconciliation in our face-to-face intimacy with the Lord, which we also lost in the Fall of man. For centuries, God told Israel, *"Seek My face"* (2 Chron. 7:14). They took this command symbolically and metaphorically because God had told Moses that "No man can see My face and live" (see Exod. 33:20). The Israelites missed God when the actual face and glory of God was revealed in the time of the Messiah through the face of Jesus Christ: *"For God...hath shined in our hearts, to give the light of the knowledge of the glory of God in the face of Jesus Christ"* (2 Cor. 4:6).

God was manifested in the flesh when Jesus came: *"And without controversy great is the mystery of godliness: God was manifest in the flesh, justified in the Spirit, seen of angels, preached unto the Gentiles, believed on in the world, received up into glory"* (1 Tim. 3:16). The Bible also confirms this when it says, *"We beheld His glory, the glory as of the only begotten of the Father"* (John 1:14). The glory that Moses asked God the Father to see was revealed in the face of Jesus Christ! Wow...what revelation! They literally found His face but missed it when they rejected Jesus.

Do you see how they missed it? We can do the same when we take one Scripture and build a theological opinion, myth, conclusion, or doctrine around one point mentioned by God in Scripture. Everything God says or does has a delicate balance to it. So, why would He say, *"No man can see Me and live"* at that moment with Moses this one time in Scripture, but in other places all throughout Scripture, say, *"Seek My face"*? I do believe that there was some metaphorical application to this command, but that doesn't mean He wasn't saying to literally seek His face. It is important to see and find the face of the Lord metaphorically, but even more so, literally. In the Old Testament, Israel understood the importance of God's countenance toward them. The Old Testament records this:

> *In the light of the king's countenance is life; and his favour is as a cloud of the latter rain* (Proverbs 16:15).

> *The Lord make His face shine upon thee, and be gracious unto thee. The Lord lift up His countenance upon thee, and give thee peace* (Numbers 6:25-26).

> *Lord, lift Thou up the light of Thy countenance upon us* (Psalm 4:6).

> *Hope thou in God: for I shall yet praise Him for the help of His countenance* (Psalm 42:5).

You see in these passages that it says the Lord's countenance or face helps us! This is why the psalmist would ask for the Lord to make His face shine, smile, or be favorable toward us, or for Him to lift up the light of His countenance upon us.

The Countenance of His Face Affects Us

God's facial expression affects us. His countenance or face serves as a strong influence and encouragement in our lives. His countenance has power in it! Just for us to stand in front of Him face-to-face one time affects us for the rest of our lives whether we realize it or not! This is why the Lord has now made His face available to us through literal face-to-face encounters with Jesus. It is important to understand the benefits of seeing Jesus. Did you know, religious preachers, pastors, and saints have had the nerve to ask me, "Why is seeing Jesus so important? What purpose or redemptive work does this accomplish?" They asked this in disbelief and skepticism, not because they don't believe that it can happen—because they are aware that the Lord does appear to individuals. Their cynicism brings an annulment to something that is so glorious, as if it's not really important. They treat seeing Jesus face-to-face as if it is in the category of miracles or signs and wonders. How erroneous that mentality is.

Experiencing Jesus face-to-face is not just a sign or a wonder; it's Him! How do you value Him? Is He just a miracle, a sign, or a wonder to you? No, my friends, He's more than that! He is God manifested in the flesh, and this is what happens when Jesus appears to you! He is God manifested in the flesh. Do you say, "No. He's only a spirit now"? After His resurrection, He appeared to His disciples in the same body and flesh that He walked the earth in, but now it was glorified.

He even had to tell the disciples this when they saw Him, for they thought He was a spirit when He appeared to them. He said, *"Handle Me, and see; for a spirit hath not flesh and bones, as ye see Me have"* (Luke 24:39). You do understand His blood was shed on Calvary and that He could not go to Heaven with a body that had flesh and blood, because the Scriptures declare that *"Flesh and blood cannot inherit the kingdom of God"* (1 Cor. 15:50). So this means He still has a body. To confirm, it says in Hebrews, *"a body has Thou prepared Me,"* and it's the same body in which He walked the seashores of Galilee (Heb. 10:5)! It's the same body in which He was raised from the dead, and it's the same body that Jesus described when He said that He was still flesh and bones (and not a spirit) when He appears to us.

"God is a Spirit," but God prepared a body for Jesus (John 4:24). He is the firstfruits of the resurrection. Jesus already has His glorified body. We, and those who have died and passed into Heaven, are waiting for the redemption of our bodies.

It is easy for Jesus to make trips from Heaven to earth in that body. He has a legal and legitimate right to appear to men in the physical realm, not just because He's God, but also because He's man. How awesome! He's the Son of God: All power was given to Him in Heaven, but after God prepared Him a body to become the Son of Man, all power is now given to Him in earth. Spirits can't be seen unless you can discern them, or see them in the spirit realm. As men, we were made with bodies here on earth to communicate, manifest, or be seen in the natural physical realm. Well, Jesus has a physical body now that is glorified and can be seen in this realm by us!

Will You Hurt the Lord by Turning Your Face From Him?

In the Bible, the Lord spoke to His people about how they had turned their face from Him. He basically described this lack of being face-to-face with Him as an act of turning their back on Him.

For they have turned their back unto Me, and not their face: but in the time of their trouble they will say, Arise, and save us (Jeremiah 2:27).

And they have turned unto me the back, and not the face: though I taught them, rising up early and teaching them, yet they have not hearkened to receive instruction (Jeremiah 32:33).

This is a strong implication! Being face-to-face with the Lord means that we turn our face to the Lord, and He turns His face to us. There are moments when we can turn our face from the Lord which includes turning our eyes, mind, ears, and mouth. All these faculties are in our face. The eyes represent our focus, the brain, the mind; the ears represent listening to Him; and His voice and the mouth speaks symbolically of our prayer life and communicating with Him. One or all of these things are included when we turn our face to the Lord. We don't understand that when we neglect the Lord in prayer—communication with Him, thinking on Him, listening to His voice by giving Him our ear and focusing on Him—that at this point we have turned our backs on Him. If your face is not turned toward Him, your back is! This is what I didn't understand in this morning visitation appearance from Jesus. I didn't know why it hurt Him so much that I had stopped spending time with Him in the mornings. Now after His heart was revealed to me in these Scriptures, I see why. Another point is that Jesus had His back turned toward me with His face looking in the opposite direction. I had never talked to Him with

His back facing me when He would appear to me. We were always face-to-face when He would come.

But this time it was different, and it hurt me because I missed being face-to-face with Him, and I knew that I hurt Him. This always bothered me after this visitation, and I knew something was gravely wrong.

Thou didst hide Thy face, and I was troubled (Psalm 30:7).

We should get troubled, just as the psalmist did, when the Lord starts hiding His face from us. It wasn't until I read the following Scripture in Jeremiah that I then understood how serious my offense was to Him.

I will shew them the back, and not the face (Jeremiah 18:17).

He hid His face from me in this visitation, and Hosea explains His heart regarding why He hides His face from us at different times:

I will go and return to My place, till they acknowledge their offense, and seek My face (Hosea 5:15).

The Bible records the Lord saying to us that He will hide His face from us and withdraw until we acknowledge our offense against Him. The Lord also lets us know in His Word that when Israel seriously offended Him, the Lord would turn His back to them and not His face. David knew how serious it was for the Lord to hide His face from us when he offended Him, and that is why he cried out in Scripture saying,

Hide not Thy face far from me; put not Thy servant away in anger: Thou hast been my help; leave me not, neither forsake me, O God of my salvation (Psalm 27:9).

Why God Hides His Face From Us

Why hidest Thou Thy face from me? (Psalm 88:14)

David wanted to know why the Lord hid His face from him at times. He knew the power of seeing the Lord's face. He did not want God to hide His face from him, for legitimate reasons. David was one of the patriarchs, and he knew the power of a face-to-face relationship with the Lord. There are several reasons the Lord mentions that explain why He hides His face from us. One of the reasons is that we offend Him in some serious way. The biggest reason from the time of Adam has been simply because of our *sin*.

My face will I turn also from them, and they shall pollute My secret place: for the robbers shall enter into it, and defile it (Ezekiel 7:22).

And the heathen shall know that the house of Israel went into captivity for their iniquity: because they trespassed against Me, therefore hid I My face from them, and gave them into the hand of their enemies: so fell they all by the sword. According to their uncleanness and according to their transgressions have I done unto them, and hid My face from them (Ezekiel 39:23-24).

And for all whose wickedness I have hid My face from this city (Jeremiah 33:5).

The Revelation of the Morning Times

Why Our Prayer Times in the Morning Are So Important to Him

It has taken me years to totally understand this visitation appearance from the Lord Jesus that only lasted a few seconds, but it was a major moment, and I didn't fully know it. I didn't catch on for years why Jesus specifically mentioned our morning times of prayer, but didn't emphasize all the other times of prayer I was having with Him. I didn't understand this because I was still spending a lot of time praying in the noon hour and in the evening time. Most people don't realize it, but God likes to follow an order and schedule, and this is not limited to the way He has organized His creation.

God Lives By His Own Word

Yes, God has created an order, pulse, rhythm, and set pattern in life, but these qualities and patterns are ones He lives by. The Lord has exalted His Word above His Name (see Ps. 138:2), and the things that He created on the earth flowed from His heart. This means He subjects who He "is" (all His Name) to what His Word says. God lives by His own Word. He places His own words, laws, and rules above the fact that He is Jehovah. He doesn't say to us, *"Well, because I'm Jehovah, I don't follow the rules that I have told you humans to live by. Because I'm God, I don't have to abide by or be accountable to the words I give mankind."* No, instead He makes Himself accountable to His own Word. Wow! How amazing! This is a great level of humility. Just think if we were as great as God. Would we actually humble ourselves to abide by the same rules and laws that we gave our subjects! God doesn't tell us to love one another, and then not love Himself. He doesn't tell us to be kind, and then not be kind Himself. He doesn't tell us to love our enemies, and then not love His enemies Himself. No, God has told us to live the way that He already lives Himself. He tells us to act the way that He does, the way that He was acting before He gave us the command.

Understanding That God's Timing and Schedule Are Different From Ours

The point is that God's schedule is different from ours. For instance, we believe a whole day consists of 24 hours. Jesus said, *"Are there not twelve hours in the day?"* (John 11:9). One full day in God's book is not a 24-hour period. To confirm this further, the Bible records timing like this, *"And it rained for forty days and forty nights"* (see Gen. 7:12). It mentions the days being 40 days and the nights being 40…the nights are identified separately from the days. The best revelation I have to explain this is from the creation story when the Lord was creating the earth. He set the pattern then: *"And the evening and the morning were the first day"* (Gen. 1:5). Wow, God called a day here on earth the time between the evening and the morning. We normally on earth calculate inaccurately, saying, "The morning until the evening is a day." How backward we are from God's time schedule. His ways are higher than our ways. This is the system Heaven is on. In reality, 6:00 P.M. at evening is the beginning of a new day. The Scripture confirms this by stating, *"the evening and the morning were the first day"* (Gen. 1:5). The Holy Spirit through the apostle Paul further confirms this when He says, *"let not the sun go down upon your wrath"* (Eph. 4:26). All unforgiveness and anger is to be settled according to this specific timing that the Bible mentions. Why? Because when the sun goes down, God views this as a new day, and God doesn't want us taking unsettled evil and angry emotions into our next day. He gives us new mercies every morning, and we should give these to others. At sunset, a new day has just begun. Do you remember the story in Genesis of the angel from Heaven wrestling with Jacob until the break of day or until dawn (see Gen. 32:24-26)? This story helps illustrate how important time is to God. The angel pointed out that a specific time marked the break of day, and the angel had to leave (see Gen. 32:26). You see, that was a significant statement, and I will explain this just a little later, but the point that I'm trying to establish is that Heaven works on a different time system than we do, and God has ordered our lives to be in line with the order that He Has ordained.

The Morning: The Most Important Part of the Day

You may ask why the morning is the most important part of the day. Well, I asked the same thing. I didn't understand it until years later when the Lord revealed to me the importance of our morning prayer time through a series of dreams and the Word. This was so awesome to me, as you will see. There are so many hidden revelations in God's Word.

This all started during a season when I felt like I was behind in ministry and concerned about God's timing for my life. Have you ever felt like this? I felt like I had missed something that God had for me through ignorance, lack of study, procrastination, and my own weaknesses. I felt like I was behind with God, but the

Holy Spirit was trying to reveal a great truth to me that would give me the victory, and redeem the time lost in my life just as He wants to do for you. The revelation came to me when He brought to my attention Job 7: 8:1-3, which answered my concerns about redeeming time. Before He brought this to my attention, He had told me to get up early in the morning. I didn't understand why He wanted me to until He led me to these Scriptures in Job. He gave me revelation about the effects of praying in the morning, especially how important it was regarding our mistakes and the mistakes of our children.

> *If thy children have sinned against Him, and He have cast them away for their transgression; if thou wouldest seek unto God betimes, and make thy supplication to the Almighty; if thou wert pure and upright; surely now He would awake for thee, and make the habitation of thy righteousness prosperous* (Job 8:4-6).

Amazing! Did you hear that! The Lord is saying that if your children have sinned in some way and God is judging them, and if you will seek God in prayer about the situation, He will awake for us, move on our behalf, and make our life prosperous.

BE UP AT DAWN AND MAKE YOUR REQUEST TO HIM.

The key point was when He said, "if thou wouldest seek unto God at betimes" (Job 8:5). Like most Christians, I didn't know what this word *"betimes"* meant, so I looked it up in the original

Hebrew context to find its meaning. I discovered that *betimes* comes from the Hebrew word *shachar*, which means, *"to be up early at dawn; at any task in the morning."*[1] At that moment, everything opened up to me about why the Lord was telling me by His Holy Spirit to get up early in the morning and pray. He was giving me the key to redeeming the time I had lost. But not even this Scripture gave me the full revelation. After this Scripture came to light, the Lord didn't stop there! For the next two to three months, the Holy Spirit gave me dreams and led me to His Word to give me the full understanding of why Jesus appeared to me about our morning times.

Morning Visitations

Be Awake—Because Here He Comes

I started reading and being led by the Spirit to study this subject. I was referencing every Scripture in the concordance on the topic of mornings when I came across the most astonishing revelation about why mornings are so significant to Jesus. It's right around the same place He led me to before in the seventh chapter of Job. The Holy Spirit gave me tremendous revelation that changed the course of my life forever! The passage says,

> *What is man, that Thou shouldest magnify him? And that Thou shouldest set Thine heart upon him? And that Thou shouldest visit him every morning...? (Job 7:17-18).*

Did you see that! There are two major points mentioned here! First, the Lord sets His heart upon us. And second, He visits us every morning—not some mornings, but *every* morning.

225

The Lord Visits Us Every Morning: He Comes During the Fourth Watch

After reading this Scripture, my eyes opened spiritually, and the Lord started talking to me, saying, "I choose to visit you on a consistent time table—every day in the morning." You see, we never find where it says anywhere in Scripture that the Lord visits men every noontime or evening. I'm not saying He can't visit us at these times of the day, because He has visited men at different times of the day. But it is the fourth watch of the morning, between 3:00-6:00 A.M. (or until dawn), that He comes and visits man on the earth. God's scheduled visitations with mankind are in the morning as the Holy Spirit declares here in the Word.

The fullness of this revelation came to me in 2006 as I studied. Now I understood why Jesus appeared to me in 1997, saying with deep hurt, "I miss the times we use to spend in the mornings." It was deeper and bigger than just missing my prayer times in the morning with Him. He was telling me that I was missing the special moment of the day when He personally comes to man on earth to visit and have fellowship. It is bigger than just prayer; it is a visitation! The mornings are His special time with me, and not only for me, but for every man or woman who will get up and meet Him at this time. Then the Lord said to me, *"David, I visit the earth every morning to fellowship with man."* He continued, *"This is one of the many different times of My visitation in man's life and in your life. I visit you daily, every morning; will you miss Me when I arrive, or will I find you asleep?"*

IT IS NOT JUST PRAYER TIME;
IT IS AN APPOINTMENT WITH GOD

My heart began racing—to know that the Almighty God and His Son Jesus visits us every morning and most of the time finds us asleep instead of awake and meeting with Him! I began understanding that I was missing my morning appointments with the Lord. I also started to understand that morning prayer was not just a prayer time, but rather it was a divinely arranged appointment with God. This stirred me to seek Him in the mornings. It also heightened my awareness on another important point that I will share shortly. The next thing He said to me was, *"David, I have a daily appointment with you every morning, and with anyone who desires a special relationship with Me."* Then He said, *"I set My heart upon you every morning. Why don't you want to be up to meet with Me when I visit?"* Then He went on to say further, *"When you get up to pray at any other time of the day, you are praying to Me on your time, not My time. My time with you is in the morning. When you get up to spend time with Me early in the morning, at dawn before the break of day, you are coming to meet Me on My time, the time that I schedule to meet with you."* Then He said, *"My time is always better, and we can get more things done."*

His Significant Works Are Done by Morning

Then He started referring to different Scriptures in my mind and heart that caused me to understand that He does every significant thing in the earth in the morning. When

Moses asked to see His glory, God responded to him that He would allow Moses to see His back parts, but not His face (see Exod. 33:18-23). But God gave Moses a requirement to meet with Him: *"And be ready in the morning, and come up in the morning unto mount Sinai, and present thyself there to Me in the top of the mount"* (Exod. 34:2). Wow! Moses says to God, *"I want to see Your glory."* God in turn tells Moses that he will have to meet God in the early morning! David the psalmist said, *"Early will I seek Thee...To see Thy power and Thy glory, so as I have seen Thee in the sanctuary"* (Ps. 63:1-2). God's power and glory are demonstrated and given in the morning times.

Jacob wrestled with the angel at the break of day, and he obtained power with God and men and was given the new name of *"Israel"* which means "a prince with God" (see Gen. 32:24-28). God raised His Son Jesus Christ from the dead early in the morning (see Matt. 28:1-7). Jesus demonstrated His power and glory by walking on the sea early in the morning during the fourth watch (see Mark 6:48). The Bible states that Jesus did most of His daily prayer very early in the morning, or that He prayed all night into the morning (see Luke 6:12; Mark 1:35)! Jesus also taught in the temple early in the morning when He walked the earth (see Luke 21:38; John 8:1-2). These Scriptures came alive, and it all began to come together for me. Then I realized that everything that God does that is significant is done early in the morning when He visits man on earth.

Visited Every Morning

Then it dawned on me that the Bible states that before Adam sinned, causing the Fall of man, the Lord visited Adam every morning to fellowship. The Bible says that the Lord came to meet Adam and walked with him in *the cool of the day* (see Gen. 3:8). Scientists will tell you that the coolest time of the day is early in the morning right before the sun rises at dawn. Another significant thing to mention is that the Bible doesn't say that two or three days passed by after Adam sinned before God came walking in the cool of the day. God would come to walk with Adam every morning. So, God came the very next morning after they ate the fruit just as He did every morning. God confronted Adam and Even the very next morning which confirms that God walked with them daily. God visited the earth and walked with Adam in fellowship every morning. *And they heard the voice of the Lord God walking in the garden in the cool of the day: and Adam and his wife hid themselves from the presence of the Lord God* (Gen. 3:8).

Three things took place when God visited Adam that also take place when He visits us!

- God speaks—"they heard His voice"
- God visits—"He came during the cool of the day" (The Morning)
- God walks—"they heard Him walking in the garden"

Jesus visits us in the morning because He models His Father. He said, "I do those things which I see My Father doing" (see John 5:19). He visits and comes walking in our garden every morning during the cool of the day. Will you hear Him walking? Will you miss the time of your visitation? Or will you take advantage of the opportunity to spend time with Him because He sets time aside to spend with you?

The Things That Belong to You When Jesus Visits in the Morning

The Scripture mentions the morning time as a time of visitation from the Lord when it states in Job, "...and visits him every morning" (see Job 7:18). From my previous study of the principles of visitations from the Lord, I knew that two main things were significant. The Lord Jesus taught us from Israel's mistakes that the two most important and significant laws of a visitation from the Lord on any level that we must observe are:

1. We are not to be ignorant of the things that will bring us peace during the visitations we have in the day in which we live (see Luke 19:42). These promises are for us today!

2. To know the timing of your visitation from the Lord. Timing is everything. How could you miss that the morning is a daily time for visitations after reading this?

Benefits of Different Types of Visitations From the Lord

You see that every visitation brings its own blessings and things that God is trying to accomplish for our peace. For example, Israel missed the time of their visitation when the Messiah Jesus Christ came to earth. Well, in that specific visitation, the Lord was trying to bring salvation to the Jews, but they rejected Him. So Jesus came to us, the Gentiles, and now we are experiencing what the Israelites should have been experiencing—salvation and redemption from sin.

Even today, if we don't receive what He did 2000 years ago, we can miss what He brought—eternal salvation, which was the main reason He came. Wow! We are still reaping even 2000 years later from a face-to-face appearance that the Lord literally gave the Jews. This should show you how powerful the benefits are from the visitations of the Lord!

If you miss the appearance of Jesus at the rapture, the consequences are that you will be left here to go through one of the worst times in history when the antichrist will invade the earth. There is no doubt that in each visitation from the Lord there are benefits and blessings that He wants to give us at that specific time. But, as Jesus told the Jews, there are also consequences for missing the time of your visitation.

Things That Belong to Your Peace in the Morning Time Visitation

The same rule applies to the daily morning visitations from the Lord. I wanted to know what belonged to our peace in these morning visitations from the Lord. I began researching this so that I didn't make the same mistake our Jewish brothers and sisters did with the Lord. Through this research, He revealed to me a number of things, and one in particular is most enlightening. As you study about morning visitations, there are things that belong to your peace that Jesus is trying to give you, but you will miss them if you miss the timing in the morning. As I researched, I found a number of places in Scripture that spoke of the things God does for us in the morning visitations.

One blessing can be in found in Lamentations: *"They are new every morning: great is Thy faithfulness"* (Lam. 3:23). He also gives us the ear and the tongue of the learned as He awakens our ears to hear Him every morning (see Isa. 50:4-5). This is powerful once you understand it. He changes our character by giving us a new name as He did for Jacob early at dawn (see Gen. 32:24-28). We receive and see His power and glory in the morning, and He shows us His glory in the morning and much more (see Ps. 63:1-2; Exod. 33:18; Exod. 34:1-2). Here are a few more things that belong to your peace in the morning time visitation:

1. He brings His justice to light every morning (see Zeph. 3:5).

2. New are His mercies every morning (see Lam. 3:22-23).

3. He promises to waken you morning by morning (see Isa. 50:4).

4. He promises to waken your spiritual ear to hear as the learned. This is the ear of the learned. He opens our ears every morning to hear Him spiritually (see Isa. 50:4-5). This learning also keeps us out of rebellion and from turning our back on Him (see Ps. 143:8). So when you wake up in the morning be expecting to hear from God (see Ps. 92:2).

5. He gives us the tongue of the learned (see Isa. 50:4-5).

6. You receive quicker transportation from God spiritually, "the wings of the morning" (see Ps. 139:9).

7. He comes seeking and looking for us by a personal visit every morning (see Job 7:18,21 and Gen. 3:8).

8. He comes walking in the cool of the day, the mornings (see Gen. 3:8; Hos. 6:3).

9. God's power and glory are shown to us (see Ps. 63:1-4; Exod. 33; 34:1-8).

10. Your nature and character of rebellion against God are changed by Him. He gives you another name as He did Jacob (see Gen. 32:24-28).

11. Your prayers will prevail with God at this time (see Gen. 32:24-28; Job 8:6).

12. He promises that you will get His attention. He will wake up for you (see Job 8:6).

13. He promises to make the habitation of your right eousness prosperous (see Job 8:6).

14. He promises to enlarge your latter end greatly. He promises to turn your small beginning into a big end (see Job 8:7).

15. He promises that joy will come (see Ps. 30:5). The joy of His way comes (see Job 8:19,21). He rejoices over us with joy through singing to us (see Zeph. 3:17).

16. He promises to send a prophet to you with a message or a prophetic message in the morning in some way (see 2 Sam. 24:11-12).

17. Seeds miraculously grow and flourish (see Ps. 90:6; Eccles. 11:6).

18. You receive power and dominion from God (see Gen. 32:24-28; Ps. 49:14).

19. God commands the morning (see Job 38:12).

20. The morning is a womb (see Ps. 110:3).

Now I've given you some of the blessings of the morning visitations in this book, but there are more, and I hope this will encourage you to go study, find the things that belong to your peace every morning, and discover what they deeply mean.

The Wings of the Morning

I said all of this to bring you to this point about how significant our morning times are with the Lord. This came to me through a dream in 2007, and the Lord used it to teach me! The Lord was in this dream, pointing His index finger at the wing of a private jet. Then He showed me a map. Then He said to me, *"When you get up to meet Me at My time early every morning, you make more progress, and you move at a faster pace with Me to your destiny, or destination in Me, than when you pray to Me at any other time of the day."* Then He continued, saying to me, *"When you get up and meet Me in prayer during the mornings, and don't miss this visitation, it's like* (then He showed me on the map) *taking a private jet from St. Louis to Texas versus taking a bus or car to get there."* He said, *"You move at a faster pace and at a quicker speed."* Then I woke up, but I didn't have scriptural proof of what the Lord had said to me in this dream. After I woke up, I asked Him, "Lord, where is the scriptural evidence for this truth You revealed to me in the dream?" Then suddenly the Holy Spirit brought a passage of Scripture that confirmed what Jesus was saying to me about this truth:

If I take the wings of the morning... (Psalm 139:9).

Then it dawned on me that the morning time is a time and space of the day in God that, in a figurative sense, has the advantage wings have over tires that move a car or bus. Suddenly, there was my answer in the Scripture. As David said (and this is what Jesus was trying to explain to me), "You can take the wings of the morning, or you can take a set of wheels which are slower." Which would you prefer? You never read anywhere else in Scripture where the Lord refers to the noon or evening times as having wings. For instance, the Bible never says wings of the noontime or wings of the evening. Wings are faster than wheels in the natural realm, and prayer is like wings in the spiritual realm. Some saints say, "I must keep the prayer wheel turning." Well, I'll rather take the prayer wings than the prayer wheels. I'll make faster progress! Wow! What revelation! This changed my life forever. The point is that Jesus visits the earth every morning. The Scripture means it when it says that God visits every morning to meet with us. Will you take advantage of this opportunity, or will you let your visitation from the Lord pass by you every morning? For you who are hungry, I think I know your answer.

ENDNOTE

1. "Shachar": see http://www.studylight.org/lex/heb/view. cgi?number=07836.

Jesus' Purpose for Appearing

The Benefits of Face-to-Face Appearances From Jesus

Jesus' Purpose for Appearing The Benefits of Face-to-Face Appearances From Jesus

One thing I have learned is that the Lord's Word is our wisdom (see Deut. 4:6). This means we can draw wisdom and understanding from the Lord about a subject by drawing or extraditing principles from the Lord's movements and actions in people's lives. In these points, I have drawn wisdom regarding the Lord's purpose in appearing to others in the past. There are just a few biblically.

1. He comes because we diligently seek Him:

   *Behold, I will send My messenger, and he shall prepare the way before Me: and the Lord, **whom ye seek, shall suddenly come to His temple**, even the messenger of the covenant, **whom ye delight in:** behold, **He shall come,** saith the Lord of hosts* (Malachi 3:1).

2. He inaugurates us as His ministers and servants:

> *...for I have appeared unto thee for this purpose, to make thee a minister and a witness both of these things which thou hast seen, and of those things in the which I will appear unto thee* (Acts 26:16).

The appearances for service: The Lord does not anoint us for spiritual picnics, and He certainly does not make a face-to-face appearance for the sake of vanity. It is all to prepare us to serve Him in some kind of capacity on earth.

3. He makes us a witness:

A.) Of the things which we have seen when He appears to us

B.) Of the things that He will appear to us about in the future

The Lord wants us to tell others that we have seen Jesus when He appears, so that we can validate His resurrection and say that He is alive.

> *And Ananias went his way, and entered into the house; and putting his hands on him said, Brother Saul, the Lord, even Jesus, that appeared unto thee in the way as thou camest, hath sent me, that thou mightest receive thy sight, and be filled with the Holy Ghost* (Acts 9:17).

4. He changes us into His image and likeness so that we can become like He is:

> *And he said, Thy name shall be called no more Jacob, but Israel: for as a prince hast thou power with God and with men, and hast prevailed... And Jacob called the name of the place Peniel: for **I have seen God face to face, and my life is preserved*** (Genesis 32:28,30).

> *But we all, with open face beholding as in a glass the glory of the Lord, are changed into the same image from glory to glory, even as by the Spirit of the Lord* (2 Corinthians 3:18).

> *Beloved, now are we the sons of God, and it doth not yet appear what we shall be: but we know that, when **He shall appear, we shall be like Him**; for we shall see Him as He is* (1 John 3:2).

5. Face-to-face appearances from the Lord preserve our lives:

> *...for **I have seen God face to face, and my life is preserved*** (Genesis 32:30).

> *In the light of the king's countenance is life...* (Proverbs 16:15).

6. Seeing the Lord face-to-face helps us. These appearances from Jesus bring the help of God with them:

*Why art thou cast down, O my soul? and why art thou disquieted in me? hope thou in God: for I shall yet praise Him for **the help of His countenance*** (Psalm 42:5).

7. Appearances from the Lord are a sign of the Lord's favor:

In the light of the king's countenance is life; and his favour is as a cloud of the latter rain (Proverbs 16:15).

8. Jesus appears to us to reveal the knowledge of the glory of His Father:

*For God, who commanded the light to shine out of darkness, hath shined in our hearts, **to give the light of the knowledge of the glory of God in the face of Jesus Christ*** (2 Corinthians 4:6).

9. Jesus appears to us to disclose to us visibly who He is as a person for the purpose of intimacy and relationship:

*He that hath My commandments, and keepeth them, he it is that loveth Me: and **he that loveth Me shall be loved of My Father, and I will love him, and will manifest Myself to him*** (John 14:21).

10. Jesus appears and comes to us to comfort us:

I will not leave you comfortless: I will come to you (John 14:18).

Then spake the Lord to Paul in the night by a vision, Be not afraid, but speak, and hold not thy peace: For I am with thee, and no man shall set on thee to hurt thee: for I have much people in this city (Acts 18:9-10).

11. He confirms and makes authentic our apostolic call:

Am I not an apostle? am I not free? have I not seen Jesus Christ our Lord? are not ye my work in the Lord? If I be not an apostle unto others, yet doubtless I am to you: for the seal of mine apostleship are ye in the Lord (1 Corinthians 9:1-2).

12. Jesus appears to us face-to-face for the purpose of showing Himself alive and risen from the dead!

To whom also He shewed himself alive after His passion by many infallible proofs, being seen of them forty days, and speaking of the things pertaining to the kingdom of God (Acts 1:3).

13. He appears to us to show us and release upon us many infallible proofs, signs, wonders, and miracles that are notable and that have never been seen. These appearances put the manifestation of the miraculous in a realm that has never been demonstrated or seen before (see Acts 1:3; John 21).

And He said, Behold, I make a covenant: before all thy people I will do marvels, such as have not been done in all the earth, nor in any nation: and all the people among which thou art shall see the work of the Lord: for it is a terrible thing that I will do with thee (Exodus 34:10).

14. The Lord appears to us to bring salvation in our lives:

But after that the kindness and love of God our Saviour toward man appeared (Titus 3:4).

15. He appears in our lives to answer our prayer requests. He appears to give us the opportunity to ask Him what we desire:

    In that night did God appear unto Solomon, and said unto him, Ask what I shall give thee (2 Chronicles 1:7).

16. When the Lord makes an appearance, it is also for the purpose of building up Zion—His Church and saints. Then He appears to edify and build up His Body—Zion; He doesn't appear for their destruction:

    When the Lord shall build up Zion, He shall appear in His glory (Psalm 102:16).

17. He appears to us to release rewards, blessings, positions of authority, and eternal crowns to us:

    And when the chief Shepherd shall appear, ye shall receive a crown of glory that fadeth not away (1 Peter 5:4).

18. He appears to inspect us (see Rev. 1-3):

    *And now, little children, abide in Him; that, **when He shall appear, we may have confidence, and not be ashamed before Him at His coming*** (1 John 2:28).

    But who may abide the day of His coming? and who shall stand when He appeareth? for He is like a refiner's fire, and like fullers' soap (Malachi 3:2).

19. Jesus appears to the Church, over which He is head, with a message from His Father (see Rev. 1-3):

    A. He is the Head of the Church.

    B. He is the Chief Shepherd over the Church at large.

20. He appears to lead and guide us where to go geographically:

    And saw Him saying unto me, Make haste, and get thee quickly out of Jerusalem.... And He said unto me, Depart: for I will send thee far hence unto the Gentiles (Acts 22:18,21).

    And the Lord appeared unto Abram, and said, Unto thy seed will I give this land (Genesis 12:7).

21. He appears to us to correct us:

    While He thus spake, there came a cloud, and overshadowed them: and they feared as they entered into the cloud. ***And there came a voice out of the cloud, saying, This is My beloved Son: hear Him*** (Luke 9:34-35).

    With him will I speak mouth to mouth, even apparently, and not in dark speeches; and the similitude of the Lord shall he behold: ***wherefore then were ye not afraid to speak against My servant Moses? And the anger of the Lord was kindled against them; and He departed*** (Numbers 12:8-9).

22. He appears to cleanse us and refine us:

> *And He shall sit as a refiner and purifier of silver:
> and He shall purify the sons of Levi, and purge them
> as gold and silver, that they may offer unto the Lord
> an offering in righteousness* (Malachi 3:3).

Visitations Versus Appearances

A visitation does not necessarily have to be an appearance from the Lord, but an appearance from the Lord is a visitation. In this book, we are talking about face-to-face appearance visitations. All appearances from the Lord are not necessarily face-to-face appearances. He can appear in His glory, meaning you will see a bright light but cannot necessarily see the complete details of the Lord's face or features.

Appearances Can Happen In Many Ways

1. *In a trance or spiritual vision:* When you are awake and either praying or in the Spirit and the Lord opens your eyes.

   A. Men who experienced Him by a vision in the spiritual realm:

   Isaiah—Isaiah 6:1-10

   Ezekiel—Ezekiel 1:1; 26-28

   Paul—Acts 22:17-21

   Peter—Acts 10:10-20

2. *In a dream:* When the Lord appears to you during deep sleep. This is also known as a night vision in the Bible.

    A. Men who experienced Him by a dream:

        Abraham—Genesis 15:12-18

        Solomon—1 Kings 3:5; 9:2

        Daniel—Daniel 7:1, 9-14

        Paul—Acts 18:9-10; 23:11

        Isaac—Genesis 26:24

        Jacob—Genesis 28:11-18; 31:11-13

        Laban—Genesis 31:11-13,29,42

3. *In the physical realm or an open vision:* When the Lord appears to you in this natural, physical world while you are awake.

    A. Men who experienced His appearance in the physical realm:

        Abraham—Genesis 18:1-3; 33

        Paul—Acts 9:1-16; 26:13-18

        John the Beloved—Revelation 1:10-20

        Daniel—Daniel 10:5-11

        John the Baptist—John 1:32-34

4. *By an out-of-body experience:* This is when your spirit is taken out of your body by the Lord to travel where He is, generally to Heaven. Flesh and blood cannot inherit the Kingdom of God, so when the Lord wants to talk to you in Heaven face-to-face, your spirit man must be sum-

moned out of your body because flesh and blood cannot exist there. When God wants to appear to you on earth, He comes down from Heaven and reveals Himself to us by appearing in a dream, open vision, in the spiritual realm, or in the physical realm.

A. Men who experienced seeing the Lord through out-of-body experiences:

Paul—2 Corinthians 12:1-9

John the Beloved—Revelation 4:1-11

5. *The glory realm:* When the Lord appears and allows you to see His splendor and magnificence from the light of His brightly shining glory.

A. Men who experienced seeing the Lord in the glory realm:

The Nation of Israel (Zion)—Psalm 102:16

Peter—Luke 9:28-32

James—Luke 9:28-32

John—Luke 9:28-32

6. *Appearances from the Father:*

A. Men who experienced Father-type appearances:

Adam (face-to-face physically)—Genesis 2:7; 3:8

Enoch—Genesis 5:24

Abraham (appearance through the disclosure of His voice by words)—Genesis 12:7; 17:1; 18:1

Isaac (appearance through the disclosure of His voice by words)—Genesis 26:2,24

Jacob (appearance in dreams by night visions)—Genesis 28:12-17

Michaiah (appearance by open vision in the spiritual realm)—1 Kings 22:19

Elijah (appearance in the physical realm)—1 Kings 19:10-14

Isaiah (appearance by open vision in the spiritual realm)—Isaiah 6:1-8

Ezekiel (appearance by open vision in the spiritual realm)—Ezekiel 1:26-28

Daniel (appearance in dreams by night visions)—Daniel 7:9-14

Moses (appearance in the glory realm)—Exodus 3:6,15-16; 19:9-20; 33:10-11; 34:1-8

Nation of Israel (appearance through the disclosure of His voice by words)—Exodus 19:9-20; Numbers 14:14

Jesus (all types of appearances)—John 1:18; 5:37

John the Beloved (appearance by open vision in the spiritual realm/out-of-body)—Revelation 4:1-11; Luke 9:33-36

Peter (appearance in the glory realm)—Luke 9:33-36; 2 Peter 1:16-18

James (appearance in the glory realm)—Luke 9:33-36

7. *Appearances from Jesus:* It is also important to know that Jesus made three physical appearances in the Old Testament to men. It was possible for Jesus to appear in the Old Testament in a physical body because the Father had prepared a body that would be sacrificed for sin from the foundation of the world. This body that Jesus came in was really prepared for Him by the Father before the world ever began (see Heb. 10:5; Rev. 13:8).

A. Men who experienced appearances from Jesus in the Old Testament:

Abraham—Genesis 18:1-33

Joshua—Joshua 5:14

Daniel—Daniel 7:13-14; 10:4-11 (compare this Scripture in Dan. 10 to Rev. 1:12-17). Note: Daniel saw Jesus twice.

Shadrach—Daniel 3:24-25

Meshach—Daniel 3:24-25

Obednigo—Daniel 3:24-25

B. Men who experienced appearances from Jesus in the New Testament:

Jesus appeared to the nation of Israel and to the whole world when He was born from a woman's womb as a man—Hebrews 10:5; 1 Timothy 3:16; 1 John 3:5

C. Those who experienced appearances from Jesus after His Resurrection—His appearance in a glorified body:

Mary Magdalene (face-to-face in the physical realm)—Matthew 28:9-10

Mary (mother of Jesus—face-to-face in the physical realm)—Matthew 28:9-10

The eleven apostles (face-to-face in the physical realm)—Luke 24:36-51; 1 Corinthians 15:5

500 men at one time (face-to-face in the physical realm)—1 Corinthians 15:5-6

Paul (out-of-body experience)—1 Corinthians 15:8; Acts 26:14-18

Stephen (open vision in the spiritual realm)—Acts 7:55-56

John the Beloved (appearances in the physical and spiritual realms)—Revelation 1:10-20

Peter (face-to-face in the physical realm)—1 Corinthians 15:5; Luke 24:34

James (face-to-face in the physical realm)—1 Corinthians 15:7

Two men on Emmaus road (face-to-face in the physical realm)—Luke 24:25-32

8. *Appearances from the Holy Spirit:* It is not a bizarre thing for the Holy Spirit to appear in person and bodily form, seeing that the two other Godheads

(The Father and Jesus) have appeared to men throughout centuries.

A. Men who experienced an appearance from the
Holy Spirit:

Jesus—Matthew 3:16-17

John the Baptist—John 1:32-33

Wisdom Concerning Appearances

1. His appearances to us are scheduled in certain places
(see Matt. 28:10).

2. Even after seeing Jesus or having an appearance from
Him, it is still possible for a man to doubt it (see Matt.
28:17).

3. It is possible for Jesus to choose a person whom He
has delivered from many devils to be His spokesper-
son, as in the case of Mary Magdalene (see Matt.
28:1-9; Mark 16:9).

4. Jesus usually appears early in the morning (see Mark
16:9; Job 7:17-18).

5. Jesus appears in different forms (see Mark 16:12).

6. It is possible for men (even godly men) not to believe that Jesus appeared to an individual (see Mark
16:10-13). We must tell others of His appearances
to us just as Jesus told Mary to (see John 20:17-18).
Moses was also commanded to tell of His appearances (see Exod. 3:15-16).

7. Jesus rebukes His leaders or apostles when they won't believe that He has appeared to others—and specifically to the ones He has sent to tell them (see Mark 16:14).

8. It is possible for our eyes to be open or closed by God when Jesus appears to us, and for us not to know that it is Him in another form (Luke 24:15-16).

9. It is possible for Him to open your eyes to see Him (Luke 24:31).

10. The telling of an appearance of Jesus can seem like an idle tale, which will cause people not to believe (Luke 24:11).

For more information about David E. Taylor, to contact the
author for speaking engagements,
or for additional copies of this book and other book titles as
well as a complete list of all products, visit:
www.kingdomofgodglobalchurch.org
or call 1-877-THE-GLORY

Send your requests to:
Kingdom of God Global Church
20320 Superior
Taylor, MI 48180

*"The Kingdom of God is the Message, Face to Face
is the Move!"*